Mc

Entertainment Weekly Top Ten
Nonfiction Book of 2008

New York Times Book Review Editors' Choice

"Hood never for a paragraph or a page loses control over the story that suffuses her, the sound of the words, the impact of images. Instead, by crafting them to be true to her own inner journey, she repeatedly breaks your heart, precisely rendering and reflecting on the aftermath of instant loss."

—*Philadelphia Inquirer*

"Hood is larger than life, living, loving and grieving on an operatic scale. . . . The book makes you hug your children tight. It makes you cry. It might even give you, as it did me, renewed respect for knitting." —*New York Times Book Review*

"*Comfort* enriches our lives. . . . I will most likely never eat pasta with butter and Parmesan or cucumbers cut in perfect rounds . . . without thinking of Ann Hood and her daughter. And I have never met either one." —*Los Angeles Times*

"In graceful prose, *Comfort* bears witness to the heartbreaking particularity of her—of any—loss."

—*People*

"Utterly harrowing, completely spellbinding. . . . Hood's spare, gorgeously serpentine narrative revisits the days and then months of almost mythical shock, comprehensive numbness, inexplicable pain, and unimaginable grief that 'funny, blonde' Grace's quick, cruel death delivered unto Hood." —*Elle*

"Hood writes . . . with harrowing candor, as a loving memorial, as a tribute to the family that did what it had to and pulled through, as the sound of a voice crying in the wilderness."

—*Boston Sunday Globe*

"'Your daughter is not going to make it.' That is unimaginable, and yet Hood re-creates it with her luminous images and hauntingly honest recounting of a mother's loss." —*Providence Journal Books*

"I do not have the greatness of heart and bare-knuckle courage to write as Ann Hood does. In our culture of hyperbole, we are told weekly about books that will 'change our lives.' But *Comfort*, Ann Hood's account of her daughter's death and her family's gutty rock climb back to wholeness is simply unprecedented, unsurpassed even by Joan Didion's *The Year of Magical Thinking*. If you read Ann Hood's true and exquisite story of unbearable loss and unforgettable love, you will be changed—not just for a week or a year but for as long as you live."

—Jacquelyn Mitchard, author of *The Deep End of the Ocean*

"Ann Hood has written an honest and eloquent memoir that goes to the marrow of grief. Seasoned with wisdom, leavened with humor, *Comfort* is a beautiful and haunting book about the most unspeakable of losses and about how comfort finds its way in from places both expected and surprising. It broke my heart and made it soar."

—Anne D. LeClaire, author of *Entering Normal* and *The Lavender Hour*

"Stunningly powerful and bravely honest, Hood's book is a brilliantly written heartbreaker that's still anchored by hope."

—*Dame Magazine*

ALSO BY ANN HOOD

Morningstar

The Book That Matters Most

An Italian Wife

The Obituary Writer

The Red Thread

The Knitting Circle

An Ornithologist's Guide to Life

Somewhere Off the Coast of Maine

EDITED BY ANN HOOD

Knitting Yarns

Knitting Pearls

Comfort

A JOURNEY THROUGH GRIEF

Ann Hood

W. W. Norton & Company

New York · London

Printed in the United States of America
First published as a Norton paperback 2009

For information about special discounts for bulk purchases, please
contact W. W. Norton Special Sales at specialsales@wwnorton.com or
800-233-4830

Manufacturing by LSC Harrisonburg
Book design by Chris Welch
Production manager: Anna Oler

Library of Congress Cataloging-in-Publication Data

Hood, Ann, 1956–
Comfort : a journey through grief / Ann Hood. — 1st ed.
p. cm.
ISBN 978-0-393-06456-8 (hardcover)
1. Grief. 2. Bereavement—Psychological aspects. 3. Loss (Psychology)
4. Children—Death—Psychological aspects. 5. Consolation. I. Title.
BF575.G7H658 2008
155.9'37092—dc22 2008001310

ISBN 978-0-393-33659-7 pbk.

W. W. Norton & Company, Inc.
500 Fifth Avenue, New York, N.Y. 10110
www.wwnorton.com

W. W. Norton & Company Ltd.
15 Carlisle Street, London W1D 3BS

2 3 4 5 6 7 8 9 0

For my family

Lorne, Sam, Annabelle, Ariane,

and Grace

PROLOGUE

Comfort

TIME HEALS.

She is in a better place.

She is still with you.

You should walk every day; you should write this down; you should go to church, to therapy, to the cemetery; these things will help you.

There is a heaven and you will see her again there.

You are not dreaming about her because you are closed to possibility.

Time heals. Once you have lived through all the firsts, it will get better. The first summer at the beach without her elaborate sandcastles; the first day of school, when she would have put on her purple leopard backpack with her collection of key chains—a starfish, miniature Lincoln Logs, the butterfly from Japan—and walked into first grade; her sixth birthday and her customary costume/painting/tea party birthday party; the first Halloween without her dressing as something with wings: an angel, a fairy, a ladybug; the first Thanksgiving when her face does not appear among the thirty others eating two twenty-three pound turkeys in our dining room; the first Christmas that I do not have to hide art supplies in the closet in my study, the bags bulging with glitter markers and crayons and sketch pads and modeling clay and watercolors and fat paintbrushes and gel pens and rolls and rolls of stickers of smiley faces and daisies and puppies and stars; the first Valentine's Day that she does not cut out construction-paper hearts and string them together for me; the first Easter without an Easter egg hunt or a pink basket filled with Smarties and Sweet Tarts and Peeps, the purple ones; the first anniversary of losing her, when the peonies are blooming in our garden and the air is filled with promise. After you have survived all of those things, it will get easier to live without her.

Are you writing down how you feel? *But I cannot write. I cannot think of anything except her, the way she looked splashing in the bathtub, the way she wiggled her toes against mine, the feel of her sticky hand holding on to my hand good and tight.* Write that down! It will help!

The images of those hours in the hospital, of the doctor's face telling you Grace was not going to make it, the rushing of nurses' feet with vials of her blood, the voice on the intercom announcing that Grace was in cardiac arrest, the way they made you wait outside the room, your face pressed against glass, the sounds of your screams, all of this will fade.

She is with you. She is a rainbow in the sky. She is the butterfly in your garden. She is the cardinal in the mimosa tree. *But I have called out her name to each of these things and they simply fade away.* That is because you don't believe.

You cannot stay in bed every day and watch *Sex*

and the City on DVD. You need to get outside. You need to walk.

You will sleep again, an entire night through. *It is when I sleep that I am back in that hospital. My own screams wake me.*

Take Benedryl, Ambien, Xanax, Zoloft, Prozac, Dr. Bach's Rescue Remedy, smoke pot, drink white wine, warm milk, single malt scotch.

Go to grief groups and listen to other parents tell how they lost their children. Then you will know you are not alone. *But when I listen to how children are dying, on go carts and in fires and with guns and falling out windows and from mistakes in hospitals, I only feel more despair.* Then you do not want to help yourself. These people can help you but you won't let them.

God loves you. *If there is a God, why would He have to take my Gracie Belle from me? Why would He do this?* God only gives us what we can bear. *But I cannot bear this.* Yes you can. You are not trying hard enough.

She is in a better place. *How can a five-year-old little girl be in a better place without her mother?* Heaven is better than here. *But she is all alone. I am all alone.*

Are you writing anything down?

Here is a book by a rabbi who lost his son; by

two women who both lost children and they have written their stories; by C. S. Lewis, who lost his wife and was Catholic and wise; by a psychiatrist, a sociologist, a teacher; by someone who has interviewed parents who lost children. *But none of them lost Grace. They do not know what it is to lose Grace.*

You need to get out of bed; off that sofa; out of the house. *The world is full of five-year-old girls. They are everywhere I go. The supermarket is full of cucumbers and blueberries and pasta. Target is full of pink dresses and purple shoes and things that sparkle and glitter and shine; the drugstore only seems to sell nail polish and hair ornaments. Out in the world there are only five-year-old girls holding their mothers' hands wherever I go.*

You should walk every day.

Aren't you feeling better? You got through a year of firsts! *I did not go to the beach this summer. I did not park in my usual place at the school so I could avoid watching the first graders filing outside through the playground at the end of the day. On her birthday I sat outside beside her toy log cabin and ate cucumbers and pasta and drank too much rosé and tried not to think about the feel of her in my arms the night she was born or how her skin was the color of apricots, while my husband talked to her best friend Adrian Roop and his mother in the dining room. I did not know what to do with her Christmas stocking, the one with the angel on it and her name sewn in my crooked attempt to use a needle and thread. I did not know how to celebrate a New Year without her. And on the first anniversary of her death, I ran away with my husband and son to Cape Cod and climbed the dunes there and felt the spring sunshine on my face as if these things could make me feel better.*

You look better!

You sound like yourself again.

Grace is sending you white feathers, heart-shaped stones, pennies from heaven.

Have you been writing this down?

I can't believe that after over a year you are still not going out more. You should be walking, taking Pilates, joining a gym. *My body cannot move. I am paralyzed.*

Here is a book about Holocaust survivors.

Did you know Winston Churchill, Abraham Lincoln, Mark Twain all lost children? And look at what they accomplished! *Then I am not as strong as they were. Grief is bigger than I am.*

Time heals.

Grace would not like you to be this way. *How do*

you know what Grace would like? I believe she would want me to miss her with every cell in my body. And that is how much I ache for her. My arms hurt from not holding her on my lap. My nose aches from not smelling her little-girl sweat and powder and lavender-lotion smell. My eyes sting from not seeing her twirl in ballet class. My ears strain every morning for her calling "Mama!" when she wakes up. My lips reach for her sticky kisses. At night I search for her.

You need to give her clothes to unfortunate children. *Even her sparkly red shoes? Her pink skirt? Her lei made of paper flowers? Her leopard rain boots? Her two-pointed brightly striped pom-pom hat?* It is not healthy to keep a shrine. *But there are shrines to lesser things. To Jim Morrison. To pets. To saints who are no longer even considered saints.* But you need to move on.

Are you writing down any of this? *Only the lies people tell me. There are no words for the size of this grief. There are only lies.*

You will see. Time heals.

In time you will sleep again and dream of beautiful things.

In time you will not miss her.

You will see.

Time heals.

Comfort

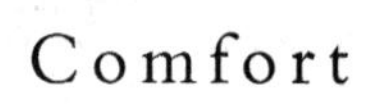

CHAPTER ONE

Losing Grace

HOW I GOT to this point, how we all did—Lorne and Sam and me—began three years earlier, on April 18, 2002. There is no hyperbole intended when I say that was the worst day of my life.

Had you asked me the day before, I would have told you that I was one of the happiest people I knew. At night, I would flop onto our oversized leopard beanbag chair with my eight-year-old son Sam and five-year-old daughter Grace and read.

Then they would climb into Sam's bunk beds, Sam on top, Grace on the bottom, and we sang Beatles songs until they fell asleep.

That is what we did one warm April night. Earlier, we had our first cookout of the year: barbecued chicken, baked beans, and corn. Sam basted the chicken while Grace dusted off our backyard furniture. She picked the purple myrtle and long green chives that grew in our backyard and made a bouquet for me. We sat in the yard, the four of us, until dusk. Then it was pajamas, the beanbag chair, and stories, a few rounds of "Eight Days a Week." Grace always got into bed with her glasses still on, and that night, as I had so many other nights, I slipped them from her still small face and said: "May I take these? Or do you need them to see your dreams?"

Forty-eight hours later, Grace was dead.

WE NAMED HER Grace three years before she was born, when I found out I was pregnant the first time, with Sam. That afternoon, driving down a winding back road in Vermont, Lorne and I decided that if we had a boy he would be Sam; a girl would be Grace. That Christmas, Lorne made an ornament for our tree that read: Sam/Grace. When I was pregnant the second time, without discussion, we knew this would be Grace.

Unlike her brother, who arrived screaming and purple, Grace was born to our favorite Simon and Garfunkel CD, quiet and calm, her skin the color of apricots. "I was your apricot and Sam was your boysenberry," she liked to say, not without smugness. Unlike her brother, she loved to sleep, taking long, cozy naps twice a day, and eager for her crib and her stuffed dog Biff early every night. Just before she fell asleep, she would lift her arms and tuck them behind her head, as if she were lying on a chaise in the warm sun.

Grace Kelly. Grace Jones. Gracie Burns. Grace Paley. Amazing Grace. It was the name of a princess, of a rock star, of a comedienne, of a writer. It was a name that inspired awe. Our Grace could be any of these things. She could be all of these things. From the minute she was born, I knew she would be.

ON APRIL 16, 2002, our son Sam turned nine years old. Lorne picked him up to take him for a "guy's afternoon"; I took Grace to her ballet class and then hurried to the local Ben & Jerry's to get Sam's birthday cake. Just that day, on the way to class, Grace told me she didn't want to do ballet in the fall, but instead wanted to take acting classes with the children's theater ensemble as Sam had done. And, she told me, she wanted to keep studying art with Don. Grace loved art most of all, and Don gave art classes that treated budding young artists with great respect and appreciation.

When I got back from Ben & Jerry's, the ballet teacher was waiting for me, frowning. Grace had fallen and seemed to have broken her arm. I ran into the class and found Grace very still, lying flat, her arm definitely at a strange angle. As I carried her to the car, she remained remarkably calm, and stayed that way even as I raced to the ER, and all through the X-rays and waiting for results. When they asked Grace to choose a face—smiley, sobbing, or in between—to express how bad she felt, she studied those pictures very seriously before she pointed to medium.

"Our little ballerina," the nurses called her as Grace was wheeled from X-Ray to a small emergency treatment room.

They took turns coming in to marvel at her, still in her ballet tights and leotard, stoically waiting to go home. Finally, she was released, her arm in a sling but not a cast. The break, they explained, was a tricky one. She might need surgery, though most likely a cast would do the trick. A pediatric orthopedic surgeon would call us the next morning. One of the nurses explained what to look for in case something called "small compartment syndrome" happened.

When she saw the look of panic cross my face, she added, "Don't worry. That won't happen. By Monday, she'll be back in school getting her cast signed."

Relieved, I gave her the *People* magazine I'd read while we waited.

While Grace was in ballet, Lorne's car was stolen out of a parking lot. "What a day," I remembered saying when he told me. That uneasy feeling of things happening in threes came to me. But I dismissed it. Sam got a ride home in a police car.

"You'll never forget this birthday!" I told him by cell phone from the hospital.

We got home late, the food for the cookout we'd planned for Sam's birthday celebration all uneaten. Instead, we ate the ice cream cake and went to bed.

"Gracie," I told her when I tucked her in.

She stopped me. "I know," she said, "I was very brave."

"You were," I said.

"I didn't like it," she said, growing teary. "I've never been in the hospital before."

"It was scary," I agreed.

That night, I crawled onto the bottom bunk, wedging myself between Grace and the wall, carefully holding her while she whimpered. Unable to sleep, I worried about whether she would need surgery, why the codeine wasn't relieving her pain. The next morning, like the day before, was unusually hot. I kept both Sam and Grace home from school, moving Grace into our big bed. Sam tried to entertain her with card tricks and jokes and singing, but she was too tired to do more than smile.

Left-handed, Sam envied that Grace had broken her left arm. "You are so lucky," he told her. "If I broke my left arm, I wouldn't be able to go to school for a month."

"I am not lucky," she grumbled. "This is awful."

With her aching arm, Grace tossed and turned uncomfortably before finally dozing off. "She needs a cast on that arm," my mother said. I called the surgeon twice, but she never called back. Frustrated, I tried to reach the ER doctor from the night before. But he didn't respond either. When I checked on Grace again, she felt feverish. Her temperature when I took it was 105. Our pediatrician advised us to go straight to the emergency room instead of to her office. Months later, I asked her why she had done that. Other mothers confessed to me after Grace died that they would have given their children Tylenol, warm compresses for their foreheads. The doctor told me, "There was something in your voice."

With his car stolen, Lorne had taken my car that day, so we had to wait for him to come and get us to go to the hospital. I sat in the back with Grace, who was—I thought—groggy with fever. Later I realized that she was slipping into unconsciousness even then.

At the emergency room, we were sent into a treatment room. Grace was given Tylenol. And then we were left alone. Lorne went down to the police station to file a report on the stolen car. Almost immediately after he left, Grace had a grand mal seizure. I had never seen one before, and wasn't even sure what was happening. I ran from the room screaming, "Help me! Someone help me!" A friend of mine with a chronically ill child once told me that a hospital's walls are lined with mothers' screams. Mine began there, in that ER.

Suddenly, we were high priority. After I convinced them she had never had a seizure before, even with fevers, they began giving her tests. X-rays, a spinal tap, an EKG, a brain wave test, blood tests. They kept eliminating horrible things: tumors, viral pneumonia, and meningitis. Her fever came down, but she didn't wake up. This was expected, they assured me. After a seizure, kids slept.

Years earlier, I had been mugged late at night in New York City. I remember running down the street and thinking that someone was talking to me, only to realize that I was actually the one talking, saying, "Don't let him kill me, don't let him kill me," a kind of prayer, I suppose.

In that hospital that night, the same thing happened. As I trotted behind the gurney wheeling Grace to one of these tests, I heard someone talking. It was me, whispering over and over, "Please wake up, please wake up, please wake up." I decided right then that all I needed was for her to look at me and say, "Mama." That would be a sign that she was all right.

Eventually, that happened. She opened her light blue eyes, her eyes the very blue of my father's, and said, "I love you, Mama." Although I cannot tell you that my knees stopped trembling then, I can say that my heart soared. "Gracie!" I said, bending to cover her with kisses.

The doctors told us she was fine. A high fever, now almost normal, had caused a seizure. She would have to spend the night. A neurologist would have to check her again in the morning. But then she would go home and be back at school by Monday. My trembling then was from relief as I held her hand all the way up to the fifth floor, where a bed and a grape Popsicle were waiting for her. A nurse told us about the great video library down the hall. She told us where we could find tea and coffee, crackers and instant soup. She brought us blankets so we could sleep there with Grace.

But all the time she spoke, I watched Grace. Her fever, monitored on a screen, was beginning to rise again. "I'll get some more Tylenol," the nurse said, cheery in her mauve uniform with teddy bears dancing across the top.

"Something's not right," I said out loud, as Grace's eyes grew distant and her Popsicle melted down its stick.

Just then, a family friend who is a doctor there stopped in to say hello. Lorne had called him during all the tests at the ER even though he's an orthopedic surgeon, not a pediatrician. On rounds that night, he decided to check in on us.

"Look who's here," I told Grace. "Andy Green." The Greens had been our friends since their daughter and Sam were three years old. But Grace didn't seem to recognize Andy at all.

He turned around, fast, and called down to the ICU. The next thing I knew, a team of doctors and nurses burst into the room, surrounding us. I looked up, and Lorne and Andy were standing in the doorway crying. "What's happening?" I screamed. Our friend could only cry and say, "Grace is very very sick."

The doctor who seemed to be in charge, barking orders at the others, looked me right in the face and said, "Your daughter is not going to make it."

I think I actually laughed at her, at the impossibility of a healthy five-year-old girl getting a fever, having all of those scary tests come back fine, and then dying. No. I laughed at her, at the impossibility of such a thing happening to my Gracie.

"We need to intubate her," the doctor barked at me.

I had watched too many television medical shows and suddenly I felt like I was in the middle of one.

"You have to help us," the doctor told me, and suddenly I was holding an oxygen mask over Grace's face and asking her to count to ten. She did. In perfect Chinese, which she studied at her kindergarten. *See how special she is,* I wanted to shout, but no one was paying attention to me.

"What is going on?" I screamed at the doctor.

But they were pushing me out of the way now, and racing with Grace suddenly hooked up to needles and machines, down to intensive care. I ran after them, yelling Grace's name. "Mama's here!" I yelled. I kept yelling even though an elevator door yawned open and took her away from me.

THERE IS A ROOM off the pediatric ICU where families wait for news. A chaplain came to us there. Then a social worker. I knew from when my father was in the hospital dying from lung cancer five years earlier that they were the staff in a hospital who prepared families for death. The room is ugly. It smells like yesterday's pizza. I could not stay there and wait, or listen to these long-faced people with their gentle voices and psychological babble.

Instead, I kept running through the automatic double doors to the doorway of the trauma room where Gracie lay, naked and vulnerable on a gurney, as people worked on her hour after hour. I saw her new pink-flowered baby doll pajamas on the floor, and I wished someone would notice them too and pick them up. She would need them when she got out of here, I told myself. Whenever someone saw me there, they would shout for me to go away. Eventually, I lay down right there, in that doorway. A nurse took me by the arms and made me get up. She found a chair for me and pushed it into the corner of that trauma room and ordered me to keep quiet.

In my flip-flops and short-sleeved shirt, I began to shiver in that cold room. Watching Grace's blood pressure drop to the point where they were losing her, then rise again; watching them try different combinations of drugs; listening to them shout, to machines beep and blare. And all I could do was watch and whisper, "Gracie, Gracie, Mama's here," from my vinyl chair in the corner. From time to time, they let my husband or me close enough to stroke her forehead, to whisper "I love you" in her ear.

At one point that same doctor looked at me and said, "This is going to be the longest night of your life." So many times after Grace died I have wanted to call that doctor, perhaps in the middle of a night, to tell her that she was wrong. In fact, that was only the first of months and months of long, endless nights, gripped by fear and grief. Nights that seemed endless. Nights that only led to mornings without Grace there.

But that night did end. And sometime the next morning, as they continued to work, I managed to catch someone's attention long enough to beg for an explanation. "What is going on? What's wrong with Grace?" No one had bothered to tell us that one of the blood tests taken the afternoon before in the ER came out positive for strep. And not just the run-of-the-mill strep that gave kids sore throats. This strep had mutated and entered her bloodstream. No one can explain why that happens. Sometimes it just does. Later we would learn that in a five-week period that spring, five children in Rhode Island and Massachusetts died from this same form of strep. Statistically, we were told, this was not unusual.

But that day, when I heard that innocuous word, I felt something like relief. Antibiotics cured strep. I knew that. But then came the worse news. The strep was not the problem. The problem was that this particular strep ravaged the organs. Even once the bacteria was under control, the damage it did was almost always fatal. I kept shaking my head, I kept saying no. I kept thinking about how two days ago Grace was making a bouquet from myrtle and chives, twirling in her tutu, showing off her latest art project.

At one point, a tall doctor came in to tell us that he needed to operate on Grace's arm. She was too fragile, he said, to move to an operating room, so he would perform the surgery right there, in the trauma room.

The tall doctor put his hand on my shoulder. "I'm going to try to save the arm," he said.

"What?" I said. I could feel the wildness in my eyes.

But he was already walking away. After an agonizing hour or more, he returned. Strep was everywhere, he said. But Grace had survived the operation.

He had used the word fragile. I knew that. But while I waited for him to return, I did not once think she might not live through the surgery. For someone who admired her own ability to listen and store information, I seemed suddenly to know nothing, to understand nothing.

Hours passed. The tall doctor came in to tell us that Grace needed another operation. This time he felt she was stable enough to go to the operating room.

"I'm going to try to save the arm," he said again.

I thought, *Grace is going to lose her arm.* She will have only one arm and it will be terrible but she will be home with us and we will figure out how to make it okay. I thought of books I'd read where children survived attacks by sled dogs or cancer of the face. Those children survived and grew up and wrote books about their experience.

I went to the waiting room to tell our families what we knew.

"What is a four-letter word for bean?" someone asked someone else, a pencil poised over a crossword puzzle.

Lima, I thought. Everything was going to be all right. I could answer questions, fill in blanks.

The next time I saw the tall doctor, he was smiling. "She did great," he said. "The arm looks good."

Relieved, I followed the gurney holding Grace back to the ICU. Her pale blond hair was pink with blood, and I took a strand in my fingers and stroked it.

"You can wash that tomorrow," a nurse whispered to me.

I nodded. Tomorrow. Grace would be here tomorrow and I would wash her hair.

Then, almost as quickly as it began, something changed. The atmosphere in the room slowed. I heard a nurse laughing.

"She's taken a turn for the better," a doctor said, in disbelief.

They showed us how pink her skin was. They boasted about her numbers: blood, kidney function, liver. A nurse explained, almost awed, how Grace would have to be in the ICU for a week or so. They would pump her with so many fluids she would look like the Michelin Man. But soon she would be transferred to a regular room. She would look like her old self again. The nurse asked if we had a picture of her, and my husband showed her the one of Grace posing in her leopard rain boots. "I never look at these until they're out of the woods," the nurse explained. They dropped her medication enough for her to answer our questions. Did she know we were there? Did she know we loved her? Was she feeling better? Yes. Yes. Yes.

I ran to the waiting room again to tell our family that she was getting better. Now they filled every chair and sofa there.

The tall doctor stopped me in the hallway. He was grinning. "Your daughter's going to be fine," he said. "I'll see you tomorrow."

Yes. Tomorrow. He would check on Grace's arm and she would be awake and her hair would have no blood in it. Then I ran back to Grace. I pulled that chair up close to her and closed my eyes. I hadn't slept in almost two days.

A doctor came in, trailed by interns who followed her like ducklings.

"A strong heart pumps good and loud," she told them. "Listen to how this one flutters. See how weak it is?"

I jumped from the chair. "No!" I shouted right in her face. "She's getting better!"

Startled, she said, "They have the infection under control. She's improving."

Each intern listened solemnly to Grace's heart. Then, without making eye contact, they all filed back out.

A nurse came in and checked this and that.

"She's all right," I said, "right?"

"Yup," she said, and turned out the light.

I kissed my daughter. I told her I was here. And I fell asleep.

Suddenly, I woke up to blaring lights and footsteps racing into the room and shouts.

I jumped from my chair, stumbling. "What's going on?"

A nurse met my eyes. "We're losing Grace," she said.

Then that doctor yelled for someone to get the mother out of here. The mother. Me.

I found my husband and the two of us watched helplessly from behind a pane of glass. Over the intercom a voice called for a cardiologist. "Grace Adrain is in cardiac arrest," the voice crackled calmly.

I beat that pane with my fists. I screamed, "Gracie! Gracie! Gracie!" so loud and so often that my throat remained dry for days afterward.

A day and a half after I carried her into the ER, Grace died.

IF WATCHING YOUR CHILD die is a parent's worst nightmare, imagine having to tell your other child that his sister is dead. Huddled on a love seat in the room Grace and Sam called the Puzzle Room because that's where we worked on jigsaw puzzles together, Lorne and I gave Sam the terrible news. Although I am certain that he cried, that we all cried, what I remember more is how we collapsed into each other, as if the weight of our loss literally crushed us.

That night, Sam slept in bed with Lorne and me, the three of us pressed together, holding on to each other tight. Day and night blurred after that first one. Finally, after a loud electrical storm sent first jagged flashes of lightning across the sky, then cold torrents of rain, the heat broke. I wandered the rooms of my house in plaid flannel pajama bottoms and turtlenecks, shivering. Sam, unable to return to his own room and the bunk beds he and Grace had so happily shared, began to sleep in the guest room or on the pullout sofa, the same place where I often spent afternoons hiding under the covers and cushions. My house, littered with Grace's artwork and clothes, no longer seemed safe. One afternoon, I wandered into Sam's room and found her ballet leotards in a tangle on the floor by the bottom bunk and her glasses on the bedside table where I had put them just a few nights earlier. "Do you need them to see your dreams?" I had asked her. Finding them made me cry, not only for Grace, but for my own innocence and hope, also lost now.

We, the three of us, moved through our lives, dazed and heartbroken. The myrtle and chives she'd picked withered. Her school brought us her unfinished kindergarten work: math papers and a kite with a long alphabet string. People planted trees in her honor, made origami cranes, drew pictures and wrote poems. But all I could do was cry, and pace the house that Grace used to call our Happy House.

CHAPTER TWO

Knitting Lessons

IN THE DAYS and weeks and months that followed, I told these details over and over to anyone who would listen. Repeating them made the story, which seemed unbelievable still, real. It was as if by repeating the details I could somehow understand them, understand what had happened to Grace, to our family.

"It was hot that day," I would say. "Remember?"

"They told us she was going to get better," I

would say, and I would describe how pink her skin had turned, how she had nodded yes when we asked her questions, how she had smiled when she heard the Beatles sing.

I told the story over and over but it still didn't make sense.

"Write it down," people told me gently.

But I couldn't write. Anything. I bought a journal and carried it around with me and sometimes I would open it and just write *FUCK* over and over again. I couldn't read either. I would stare at a page in a magazine, or a letter someone wrote to me, and the words simply did not make sense. My brain couldn't settle on any one word long enough to form it.

After a while, I began to read the newspaper again, especially the obituaries. I started to cut phrases out of them that struck me, and I imagined making poems about death and loss by piecing together all of these random phrases about people who had died. I never did that. But I kept collecting them. I read the *National Enquirer* too, forgetting as soon as I read them the details about movie stars' lives.

Then, one summer night over a year after Grace died, I checked my e-mail and found one from Rob Spillman at Tin House soliciting essays and fiction for a theme issue on lies. Right then, I opened a new Word file for the first time since Grace had died and I wrote what is now the prologue for this book. I wrote it in one sitting. Then I went to bed. The next morning, I read what I wrote and I started to cry. This was what had happened. This was what I knew. And I had, finally, written again.

BEFORE GRACE DIED, I could not imagine my life without writing. I put myself to sleep by making up stories. I carry characters and plots around with me the way other people carry their lipsticks and hairbrushes: they go everywhere I go. Sitting at my computer, staring at my own words on the screen, I wondered how I had made it this long without words. Then I realized.

Knitting saved my life.

If ever a life needed saving after loss, it was mine. In the past, when grief struck or my heart was broken, I had always turned to words. Reading and, later, writing never failed to help me escape from and heal the wounds life inflicted. As a fiction writer and essayist, I had published many books and articles that explored life's heartaches and challenges. But Grace's death was too enormous, too sudden, too hard to grasp. One day she was a vibrant little girl twirling in her ballet class; two days later she was dead.

Of course, I did turn to books for consolation. Friends delivered volumes of poetry and books on grief by the dozen. But when I tried to read, letters no longer formed words, and words did not make sentences. Instead, each page held a jumble of letters that meant nothing, no matter how hard I stared.

That summer, we decided to go to a wedding in San Francisco that we had planned to attend before Grace died. One of the difficult tasks we'd had to complete was getting a new car since our stolen one had been totaled. Imagining a future when we would once again take family road trips, we bought a VW Euro van in metallic green. It looked sad and empty to me, with Sam alone in the big backseat and the promise of fun seeming impossible. But we had taken it to beaches and mountains, to drive-ins and campgrounds, opening the screens to fill it with fresh air, popping the top and lowering the backseats to make beds. Briefly, we imagined driving to the wedding. But like most plans that summer, that one seemed insurmountable. Instead, we decided to rent a VW van in San Francisco and drive it all the way to Seattle and back.

Camping on beaches and navigating sand dunes, the rocky landscape and rough surf, all seemed somehow to reflect our loss. We arrived in Portland, Oregon, to visit our friends Heather and Hillary, and to meet Hillary's fiancé. They fed us and comforted us and even made us laugh. One day, I went out for a walk with Heather and Hillary and started to cry. What a betrayal, I said, to have words abandon me now, when I needed them more than ever.

"Go and learn to upholster a couch!" Hillary said.

I frowned at the suggestion. I was clumsy with needles and thread and had no sense for fabrics or colors.

But they both persisted. "Do something with your hands."

I explained how my hands used to sweat in home economics when it was time to pin the pattern to the fabric; how I snuck home my paisley-print coulottes for my cousin to add the zipper; how, during college, in a fit of love and passion, I spent months needlepointing a pillow for a boy. It came out so crooked that I vowed never to waste my time again.

LEARNING TO KNIT had never occurred to me before Grace died. Needles, thread, yarn, scissors, all belonged to a world that was not mine. When a button fell off a coat, it stayed off. When pants needed hemming, I paid a tailor to do it.

That fall Sam returned to the distraction of fourth grade. Lorne went back to his office, and although he often felt unable to work, his old routines and the needs of his clients kept him busy. Unable to write, I faced the loneliness of every day at home without Grace.

On one such day, desperate, I opened the Yellow Pages and called knitting stores to sign up for a beginners' class. But I had missed the start of most of them, and the others were held at night, when I wanted nothing more than to hold Sam and Lorne close to me. One afternoon, as I waited for Sam at his school, a friend of a friend ran up to my car, thrust a piece of paper into my hand, and said, "Call Jen. She'll teach you how to knit."

I learned to knit while sitting in the corner of a busy yarn shop in a seaside town thirty miles from my Providence home. Jen, who ran Sakonnet Purls, her mother's yarn store, with humor and cool efficiency, patiently talked me through the basics. Even after she explained, "Knitting is a series of slipknots," and I looked up at her in total bewilderment, she never grew impatient. However, when I stood up to leave, two hours had passed, the first two hours in months that I hadn't spent crying or cursing or reliving the horrible tragedy that had taken over my life.

A week later, I was struggling through a scarf. I made a mess of it, randomly adding stitches, dropping stitches, then adding even more. When I showed up with this tangle of wool, Jen pulled it off the needle and all my mistakes were miraculously gone. I could start anew. Unlike life, or at least this new life of mine—in which I was forced to keep moving forward through the mess it had become—knitting allowed me to start over again and again, until whatever I was making looked exactly as I wanted it to look.

Soon I became a voracious knitter. I bought more yarn, a crazy variegated self-striping ball of yellow, pink, and purple, and began to knit whenever stress or my overactive grieving brain took over. Which is to say that I knit all the time—in the grocery store parking lot, at the kitchen table, on car trips while my husband drove, even when those car trips went into the night. "What?" knitting guru Elizabeth Zimmermann wrote in her book *Knitter's Almanac*. "You can't knit in the dark? Stuff and nonsense; anybody can."

There were many days when all I did was knit. Once, after nearly eight hours of knitting, I could not even open my cramped fingers. I knit scarves and hats and socks, and as I knit, every part of me calmed. The quiet click of the needles, the rhythm of the stitches, the warmth of the yarn and the blanket or scarf that spilled across my lap, made those hours tolerable. I made a red hat for Lorne, a blue one for Sam. I knit my cousins fluttery scarves for Christmas, and for myself a scarf in Grace's favorite colors: pink and purple. I began a sweater. I learned to read a pattern, to decipher the language of knitting. It quieted the images of Grace's last hours in the hospital. It settled my pounding, fearful heart.

One morning, as I lay in bed trying to figure out how to face another day, my phone rang. The woman on the other end told me her daughter had gone to school with Grace. As soon as I heard this tenuous connection, I wanted to hang up the phone. Wasn't anyplace safe? Here in my bed, in my home, I had to revisit what I so desperately couldn't handle? But, sensing the change of tone in my voice, the woman spoke hurriedly. Her own two-year-old son had died, she said, and I heard myself saying the words so many people had said to me: What happened?

I understood the comfort in the repetition of the story. As she told me every detail, I got out of bed and began to pace: up the stairs, down the stairs, across each silent room of my house. Her words sent me into my own senseless movements. As soon as we hung up, I collapsed into a chair and began to knit. But first, I made a date with her: Come to my house, I told her. I will teach you how to knit. Knitting is the only comfort I can offer.

For me, knitting is like meditation. It is not that my mind numbs or goes blank; in a way, the complete opposite happens. If I stop paying attention, I make a mistake. I confess that I love to knit while cooking shows play on my television. Knitters I know knit to all kinds of music, from classical to show tunes. But as soon as we pick up our needles, we enter that still place. Our attention becomes specific to what is in our hands and the outside world fades away.

Even now, I sometimes drive those thirty miles to Sakonnet Purls for a knitting lesson. Jen has moved to Chicago, and someone new runs the class. Six or eight or ten women sit in a circle, on sofas and chairs, and knit. We don't talk much. I concentrate on manipulating four tiny needles to make a pair of socks. Our heads bent, from time to time someone moans, "Oh no!" or shares her measuring tape or sighs in satisfaction. Here I am just another person who loves to knit, not the woman whose daughter died. I am anonymous. Last week, a woman said, "I read somewhere that knitting is good for depression." I kept my head down, even as I thought, *If you only knew . . .*

There is a story in Ann Feitelson's book *The Art of Fair Isle Knitting* about a storm that took the lives of eight Shetland Islands fishermen in 1897. She writes that the women left behind, stricken with grief, supported themselves by knitting. "Focusing on the knitting in one's lap," Feitelman writes, "keeps death and uncontrollable forces at bay."

Now I am kin to those women in Shetland, and to all those who find in the rhythm of the needles, the precision of our stitches, the weight of the wool, a way to keep death at bay, at least for a few rows.

In her poem "Wage Peace," Judyth Hill writes:

Learn to knit, and make a hat.

Think of chaos as dancing raspberries,
imagine grief
as the outbreath of beauty
or the gesture of fish.

Swim for the other side.

Slowly, words began to return to me. I still struggled to finish reading a book, or to write a page. But every day I picked up my knitting needles. I cast on, counting my stitches. Then I swam, Gracie. I tried to swim to the other side of grief.

CHAPTER THREE

Comfort Food

GRIEF IS NOT LINEAR. People kept telling me that once this happened or that passed, everything would be better. Some people gave me one year to grieve. They saw grief as a straight line, with a beginning, middle, and end. But it is not linear. It is disjointed. One day you are acting almost like a normal person. You maybe even manage to take a shower. Your clothes match. You think the autumn leaves look pretty, or enjoy the sound of snow crunching under your feet.

Then a song, a glimpse of something, or maybe even nothing sends you back into the hole of grief. It is not one step forward, two steps back. It is a jumble. It is hours that are all right, and weeks that aren't. Or it is good days and bad days. Or it is the weight of sadness making you look different to others and nothing helps. Not haircuts or manicures or the Atkins Diet.

Writing about Grace, losing her, loving her, anything at all, is not linear either. Readers want a writer to be able to connect the dots. But these dots don't connect. One day I think about how knitting saved my life, and I write about that. But how do I connect it to other parts of my grief? Grief doesn't have a plot. It isn't smooth. There is no beginning and middle and end.

Stories demand order, someone told me. But I no longer live an orderly life. I used to. For example, every day at five o'clock I cooked my family dinner. I planned it ahead of time. I squeezed melons and chose green beans and asparagus with care. I shopped for good cuts of meat on sale. I thought about food groups, balanced diets, flavors and colors that worked together.

These are the things I remember:

Grace loved cucumbers sliced into perfect circles, canned corn, blueberries, any kind of beans, and overripe kiwi. A family vacation to southern Italy had left her with a taste for lemons and kumquats. She carried hard dried salami in a small pink and white gingham purse and liked to go with me to Italian delis for fresh buffalo mozzarella. Her favorite dinner was pasta—*noonies,* we called it, a leftover mispronunciation from Sam when he was a baby—with butter and freshly grated Parmesan cheese. Every day she took the same thing for her school lunch: prepackaged cheese and crackers, those cucumber rounds, half-sour pickles. When her friend Adrian came over for lunch they always ate Campbell's chicken and stars soup, Ritz crackers, and either pomegranate or kiwi. "Ade is coming today," she'd remind me. "Don't forget the pomegranate."

While I cooked dinner, Sam and Grace both helped me. They layered the potatoes for potatoes au gratin—*cheesy* potatoes in our house; they peeled the apples for apple crisp, the carrots for lentil soup; they shook and shook and shook chicken in a baggie of seasoned flour for chicken marsala. Grace used to like to press her thumbprint onto peanut butter cookies to flatten them before baking.

These are the things I remember: a fire in our kitchen fireplace, soup simmering on the stove, Sam and Grace bursting in with their cheeks red, their snowsuits wet, dripping snow across the wooden floor to snack on pickles straight from the jar before heading back outside.

Or: our first backyard barbecue of the year on a surprisingly warm April day, Sam at eight finally old enough to baste the chicken on the grill, Grace carefully wiping a winter's worth of dust from the patio table and chairs, paper plates decorated with red cherries, the smell of molasses and brown sugar from the pot of baked beans, a bowl of canned corn dotted with butter, late afternoon sunshine, the purple heads of crocuses announcing themselves in our small garden.

The spring that Grace died, I remember that April remained relentlessly warm and sunny, but inside our house I shivered uncontrollably. Wrapped in flannel blankets and shawls from visitors, I could not find comfort. This was the unthinkable, the thing every parent fears. And it had come to our house and taken Gracie. When I looked out the window, I wanted her to still be there, making bouquets of chives from the garden laced with purple myrtle. Or when I walked in the kitchen, I expected to find her there, standing on her small wooden chair, plucking one cucumber round after another from her pink plate into her baby-teeth-filled mouth.

People brought food. Chicken enchiladas in a throwaway foil roasting pan and rich veal stew simmering in a white Le Creuset pot and cold cuts and artisan breads and potato salad and fruit salad and miniature tarts and homemade chocolate chip cookies and three different kinds of meat loaf and three different kinds of lasagna and chicken soup and curried squash soup and minestrone soup. It was as if all of this abundance of food could fill our emptiness.

We sat, the three of us left behind, and stared at the dinners that arrived on our doorstep each afternoon. We lifted our forks to our mouths. We chewed and swallowed, but nothing could fill us. For months people fed us, and somehow, unimaginably, time passed. Summer came and friends scattered to beaches and foreign lands.

One day, gourmet ravioli filled with lobster and a container of vodka cream sauce appeared on our doorstep with a bottle of Pinot Grigio. Our garden was in full bloom by now. Hot pink roses. Ironic bleeding hearts. Columbine, and unpicked chives topped now with purple flowers. I carried the bag into my quiet kitchen and thought through the steps for cooking pasta. The process that had once been automatic had turned complicated. *Get a pan*, I told myself. *Fill it with water.* I had not done even these simple things in almost three months. Yet soon the water was at an angry boil, the sauce simmered in a pan beside it. The simple act of making this food felt right.

The next day, I once again set a pot of water to boil. But instead of expensive pasta, I filled it with the medium shells that Grace had loved. When they were al dente, I tossed them with butter and parmesan cheese. That night, as the three of us sat in our still kitchen, the food did bring us comfort. It brought Grace close to us, even though she was so far away. Crying, I tasted the sharp, acrid tang of the cheese. It was, I think, the first thing I had tasted in a long time.

We think of comfort food as those things our mother fed us when we were children. The roast chickens and mashed potatoes, chocolate cream pies and chewy brownies. But for me now, comfort food is cucumbers sliced into circles. It's chicken and stars soup with a side of kiwi. It's canned corn heated to just warm. In losing Grace, there is little comfort. But I take it when I can, in these most simple ways. On the days when grief grabs hold of me and threatens to overtake me again, I put water on to boil. I grate parmesan cheese and for that night, at least, I find comfort in a bowl of noonies.

Not long ago, I was in the supermarket and a small basket of bright orange kumquats caught my eye. I remembered that long-ago trip to Italy when Grace developed a taste for this funny fruit. I could almost picture her in the front seat of my shopping cart, filled with delight at the sight of kumquats. I reached into the basket of fruit and lifted out one perfect kumquat, small and oblong and orange. When I bit into it, tears sprang into my eyes. The fruit's skin is sour, and it takes time before you find the sweetness hidden inside.

CHAPTER FOUR

Now I Need a Place to Hide Away

I WANT TO connect things. But how do I connect, for example, knitting and cooking and tattoos and the Beatles? All of these things are important to my story, to my grief, to losing Grace. But I don't have a timeline:

August 2002: cooked pasta again for the first time.

October 2002: learned to knit.

I am struggling to put things in order. For example, September 24, 2002. Grace's sixth birthday.

My three cousins and I piled into a car and drove across town to the Federal Hill Tattoo Parlor. Until that day, my experience with tattoos was pretty limited. My father had one on his forearm, a giant blue eagle in front of a red sun with the letters *USA* across the bottom. I used to trace its outline when I sat on his lap, the colors already dull and faded. When he was fourteen, he ran away from home and got the tattoo at a carnival in rural Indiana. In college, a group of boys my friends and I palled around with got drunk one night in Newport and got tattoos on their hips. They stumbled into the dorm and lowered the waistband on their jeans to show off the swollen, tender designs: a sea horse, a devil, a grinning leprechaun. The students who live in my neighborhood have tattoos peeking out from shirtsleeves and necklines and the cuffs of their pants.

But I was not running away from home, or drunk, or rebelling. I was getting a tattoo as a constant reminder of Grace. It had been five months since Grace died. In her own words, she was five and seven-twelfths that April. In the past, she had planned her own elaborate birthday parties. For her third birthday she had a tea party; for her fourth, a costume party. On her fifth birthday—her last one—she gathered her friends into a parade and marched around the neighborhood singing "Happy Birthday." Now, her sixth birthday arrived without her to celebrate it.

Birthdays of a child who has died are strange events. How can a mother ever forget the joy of that day? Her first glimpse of her baby? The lightness of a newborn in her arms? Grace was born on F. Scott Fitzgerald's one hundredth birthday. She weighed six pounds three ounces, and already had the blue eyes that the doctor announced were "keepers" and wouldn't change color. Her skin was the color of apricots. On all of her birthdays, including this most terrible one, I remembered how my labor began at dawn; how my father brought me his homemade stew for lunch; how, at the hospital, I spent an hour in a bathtub, then got out, dried off, and delivered my beautiful daughter twenty minutes later.

Grace's birthday dinner was always sliced cucumbers and shell pasta with butter and parmesan cheese. I had planned to have that dinner this year too, and rosé because pink was her favorite color. But somehow it didn't seem enough. I needed to do something more, something that would last beyond this one day. When I decided that getting a tattoo was the perfect way to mark my daughter's birthday, even the knowledge that it would be painful seemed right.

In the tentative way that people approach a grieving mother, my cousins asked what I needed to help get through Grace's birthday. As I told each one what I had decided to do, they decided to come with me and get tattoos too. On that sunny Saturday afternoon, we walked into the tattoo parlor and studied the books of designs. There were Chinese symbols and pinup girls and butterflies; broken hearts and beating hearts; flags, cars, scrolls, and skulls. But nothing seemed right.

Melissa, the youngest of us and already boasting three tattoos, came up with the idea of a bell. A small pink bell at the ankle in honor of Grace's self-proclaimed nickname, Gracie Belle, and her brother Sam called her Miss Belle. A bell was perfect. But in all of those books, there were no bells. So Gloria-Jean, the oldest of us, drew a bell for the tattoo artist. Her pen hesitated a moment, and then she added two small lines at the bell's edge. These bells were ringing, and they would keep ringing.

As I lay on the table, my eyes squeezed shut, I could not help but think of six years earlier, when I had laid down to bring Grace into the world. The needle buzzed and pierced my skin, sending burning pain though me. I felt myself begin to cry. "How bad is it?" Cousin Gina called to me. I swallowed hard, thinking of the pain of childbirth, the pain of loss. "Not bad," I told her. "Not bad at all."

I have now passed as many birthdays without Grace as I did with her. I still serve shell pasta with a side of cucumbers on that day. I still pour rosé. I still remember how happy I was when I first held her in my arms, the way she looked up at me with a calm that newborns usually don't possess. Once a year, on her birthday, I let myself feel that painful joy of having had Grace, and having lost her too soon. But every day, every single day, I look down the length of my leg to the inside of my ankle where that small pink bell sits, still ringing.

YES. I LEARNED to knit.

I got a tattoo.

But mostly what I did was hide. I hid from people who maybe didn't know what had happened. One day, Sam and I were in CVS and we saw à woman whose daughter had played soccer with Sam when they were both about four years old. Her younger daughter was named Grace and was the same age as our Grace. Sam stopped playing soccer after a year or so. I hadn't seen the woman since. But now here she was in CVS with her daughters, her Grace. I crouched behind giant rolls of paper towels. I ran up an aisle as she entered it. My heart was beating fast while the sound of her voice floated across the store. Sam held my hand tight, unsure of why I was acting this way. He was getting used to my hiding. The week before I had hid behind my car to avoid a woman I knew pumping gas across from us. One day I practically jumped under the table at our local diner to avoid eye contact with two ballet moms whose daughters had arabesqued with Grace since they were all three.

I hid from everything.

But it is difficult to hide from the Beatles. After all these years they are still regularly in the news. Their songs play on oldies stations, countdowns, and best-ofs. There is always some Beatles anniversary: the first No. 1 song, the first time in the United States, a birthday, an anniversary, a milestone, a Broadway show. Just today I opened a newspaper to a review of a new movie about John Lennon.

But hide from the Beatles I must. Or, in some cases, escape. One day in the grocery store, when "Eight Days a Week" came on, I had to leave my cartful of food and run out. Stepping into an elevator that's blasting a peppy Muzak version of "Hey Jude" is enough to send me home to bed.

Of course it wasn't always this way. I used to love everything about the Beatles. As a child I memorized their birthdays, their tragic life stories, the words to all of their songs. I collected Beatles trading cards in bubble gum packs and wore a charm bracelet of dangling Beatles' heads and guitars.

For days my cousin Debbie and I argued over whether "Penny Lane" and its flip side, "Strawberry Fields Forever," had been worth waiting for. I struggled to understand "Sgt. Pepper"; I marveled over the brilliance of the White Album.

My cousins and I used to play Beatle wives. We all wanted to be married to Paul, but John was okay too. None of us wanted Ringo. Or even worse, George.

It was too easy to love Paul. Those bedroom eyes. That mop of hair. Classically cute. When I was eight, I asked my mother if she thought I might someday marry Paul McCartney.

"Well, honey," she said, taking a long drag on her Pall Mall, "somebody will. Maybe it'll be you."

In fifth grade, in a diary in which I mostly wrote, *It is so boring here,* or simply, *Bored,* only one entry stands out: *I just heard on the radio that Paul got married. Oh, please, God, don't let it be true.*

It was true, and I mourned for far too long.

Of course by the time I was in high school, I understood my folly. John was the best Beatle: sarcastic, funny, interesting-looking. That long thin nose. Those round wire-rimmed glasses. By then I didn't want to be anybody's wife. But I did want a boy like John, someone who spoke his mind, got into trouble, swore a lot, and wrote poetry.

When I did get married and then had children, it was Beatles songs I sang to them at night. As one of the youngest of twenty-four cousins, I had never held an infant or babysat. I didn't know any lullabies, so I sang Sam and Grace to sleep with "I Will" and "P.S. I Love You." Eventually Sam fell in love with Broadway musicals and abandoned the Beatles.

But not Grace. She embraced them with all the fervor that I had. Her taste was quirky, mature.

"What's the song where the man is standing, holding his head?" she asked, frowning, and before long I had unearthed my old "Help!" album, and the two of us were singing "You've got to Hide Your Love Away" together.

For Grace's fourth Christmas, Santa brought her all of the Beatles' movies on video, a photo book of their career, and the *Beatles 1* tape. Before long, playing "Eight Days a Week" as loud as possible became our anthem. Even Sam sang along and admitted that it was arguably the greatest song ever written.

Best of all about my daughter the Beatles fan was that by the time she was five she had already fallen for John. Paul's traditional good looks did not win her over. Instead she liked John's nasally voice, his dark side. After watching the biopic *Downbeat,* she said Stu was her favorite. But since he was dead, she would settle for John.

Once I overheard her arguing with a first-grade boy who didn't believe that there had been another Beatle.

"There were *two* other Beatles," Grace told him, disgusted. "Stu and Pete Best." She rolled her eyes and stomped off in her glittery shoes.

Sometimes, before she fell asleep, she would make me tell her stories about John's mother dying, how the band met in Liverpool, and how when Paul wrote the tune for "Yesterday," he sang the words "scrambled eggs" to it.

After I would drop Sam off at school and continue with Grace to her kindergarten, she'd have me play one of her Beatles tapes. She would sing along the whole way there, replacing the word "yesterday" with "scrambled eggs."

On the day George Harrison died, Grace acted as if she had lost a friend, walking sad and teary-eyed around the house, shaking her head in disbelief. She asked if we could play just Beatles music all day, and we did. That night we watched a retrospective on George. Feeling guilty, I confessed that he was the one none of us wanted to marry.

"George?" Grace said, stunned. "But he's great."

Five months later, on a beautiful April morning, Grace and I took Sam to school, then got in the car and sang along with "I Want to Hold Your Hand" while we drove. Before she left, she asked me to cue the tape so that as soon as she got back in the car that afternoon, she could hear "You've Got to Hide Your Love Away" right from the beginning. That was the last time we listened to our Beatles together.

The next day Grace spiked that fever. Briefly, as she lay in the ICU, the nurses told us to bring in some of her favorite music. My husband ran out to the car and grabbed *1* from the tape deck. Then he put it in the hospital's tape deck, and we climbed on the bed with our daughter and sang her "Love Me Do." Despite the tubes and machines struggling to keep her alive, Grace smiled at us as we sang to her.

At her memorial service, eight-year-old Sam, wearing a bright red bow tie, stood in front of the hundreds of people there and sang "Eight Days a

Week" loud enough for his sister, wherever she had gone, to hear him.

That evening I gathered all of my Beatles music—the dusty albums, the tapes that littered the floor of my car, the CDs that filled our stereo—and put them in a box with Grace's copies of the Beatles' movies. I could not pause over any of them.

Instead I threw them in carelessly and fast, knowing that the sight of those black-and-white faces on *Revolver,* or the dizzying colors of *Sgt. Pepper,* or even the cartoon drawings from *Yellow Submarine,* the very things that had made me so happy a week earlier, were now too painful even to glimpse.

As parents do, I had shared my passions with my children. And when it came to the Beatles, Grace had seized my passion and made it her own. But with her death, that passion was turned upside down, and rather than bring joy, the Beatles haunted me.

I couldn't bear to hear even the opening chords of "Yesterday" or a cover of "Michelle." In the car I started listening only to talk radio to avoid a Beatles song catching me by surprise and touching off another round of sobbing.

I tried to shield myself from the Beatles

altogether—their music, images, conversations about them—but it's hard, if not impossible. How, for example, am I supposed to ask Sam not to pick out their music slowly during his guitar lessons?

Back in the sixties, in my aunt's family room with the knotty-pine walls and Zenith TV, with my female cousins all around me, our hair straight and long, our bangs in our eyes, the air thick with our parents' cigarette smoke and the harmonies of the Beatles, I believed there was no love greater than mine for Paul McCartney.

Sometimes now, alone, I find myself singing "I Will" softly. I sing to Grace, imagining her blue eyes shining behind her own little wire-rimmed glasses, her feet tapping in time. It was once my favorite love song, silent now in its White Album cover in my basement.

How foolish I was to have fallen so easily for Paul while overlooking John and George, to have believed that everything I could ever want was right there in that family room of my childhood: cousins, TV, my favorite music. But mostly I feel foolish for believing that my time with my daughter would never end.

Or perhaps that is love: a leap of faith, a belief in the impossible, the ability to believe that a little girl in a small town in Rhode Island would grow up to marry Paul McCartney. Or for a grieving woman to believe that a mother's love is so strong that the child she lost can still hear her singing a lullaby.

CHAPTER FIVE

Wildfires

WHEN I TRY to find order in the chaos of grief, those are the things that occur to me. The darkness of the tattoo parlor. How the tattoo bled while I sat with my cousins in my backyard on that first birthday of Grace's after she died. I was hiding then too. Inside sat her friend Adrian's parents, invited by my husband, who didn't realize how painful it was for me to see them again. I see myself singing a Beatles song with such desperation that it hurts for me to remember it. Sometimes now I run my fingers over all the yarn I bought to prevent myself from running out. What if one night I knit my way through all I had and then had to sit without being able to knit anything? So I bought more than anyone could ever use. I bought so much yarn that we converted a small room in our house to a knitting room, one wall filled with shelves to hold all the yarn.

We took that road trip that summer, driving the rented VW van from San Francisco to Seattle and back. Hillary had just gotten engaged, I think. Her wedding was the following summer, 2003. This time we could manage to organize a cross-country trip in our own VW van. We drove from Providence to Oregon and then from Oregon home.

Wildfires surrounded the Black Butte Ranch the weekend of Hillary's wedding. Evacuation routes hung from trees, bright orange, pointing the way to safety. An AM radio station gave updates as the fires moved in on us, growing closer and closer.

Afraid to unpack, we left our luggage by the door of the condo we'd rented on the property.

Without the haze of smoke and the bitter taste it brought with it, we would have a beautiful view of the Cascade Mountains, towering Ponderosa pines, the silvery leaves of aspens. But when we stood on the deck, we only saw smoke growing denser as the fires moved toward us.

As a distraction, my husband and I took Sam to the swimming pool. The nervous wedding party and other guests lounged poolside under the thick gray skies. I jumped into the water beside Sam. When my head popped out, I saw ash floating on the surface. Ash showered down on us. There was ash in people's hair and dusting their tanned shoulders. I thought of Pompeii, of the world coming to an end.

Hillary, the bride, our former nanny, appeared, giggling and golden blonde, dreamy-eyed and hopeful even as fire threatened. She was not thinking that plans could go awry, that catastrophe loomed around every corner. She was optimistic, her new life about to unfold amid this ash and these mountains. Why shouldn't she be optimistic? Why shouldn't she believe the fires would change direction and spare her?

I bent my head so that no one would see me cry. I was at a wedding, I reminded myself. I was surrounded by happiness, by happy people, even if that part of me, the happy part, had disappeared. It was on hold in the year since Grace had died.

Hillary had been Grace's first nanny, living with us for three years. She had been there the day I went into labor with Grace, and the day that I brought her home from the hospital. She had carried Grace all around Providence in a backpack, the two of them chattering to each other as they went out for adventures. And Hillary had flown to my side when she learned that Grace had died. Without hesitation, she had traveled from her home in Portland and stayed with us, her pockets full of pictures she had of Grace.

My crying grew stronger. For me, Grace and Hillary were linked in a special way. But now here was Hillary about to be married, and we had lost Grace. Time was moving forward, taking us even farther away from the days when my family was happy and complete. I caught sight of Hillary, her head tossed back in laughter, and the ache of my loss overcame me. I dunked myself back under the water. My eyes open, the blue shimmered around me. Above, the bits of ash floated like confetti.

HILLARY CAME INTO my life on a bright summer afternoon in 1996. She was tall and skinny with a tattoo on her ankle. She had hair dyed bright red and cut real short. If Princess Diana were an art student, she would have been Hillary: they shared the same nose, the same posture, the same awkward smile. Hillary came that day to talk to us about the position of a live-in nanny that we had posted on the jobs board at the Rhode Island School of Design.

Lorne posted our ad. Before he even left the employment office, he had met a twenty-eight-year-old returning student, an apparel design major from Portland, Oregon. She was only here for the summer, she explained. Then she was leaving for an internship in Paris. They made a time for her to come over to our house to talk.

As Lorne walked out the door, another woman ran toward him. She was also twenty-eight years old, also a returning student, also an apparel design major, and also from Portland, Oregon. But she was going home for the summer, and was interested in beginning in September. Her name, she told him, was Hillary.

WHEN I WAS a little girl, I had a fantasy. It was not to be a ballerina or a movie star, or even a writer. My fantasy was to live in a big house like the one on the TV show *Please Don't Eat the Daisies,* and to have a lot of children and a big dog and a messy office where I would try to write novels. I liked the happy noise in that fantasy. I liked the chaotic household, the wry, witty mother, the mischievous children.

At the time Hillary came into my life, I thought I was on my way to that fantasy. After many happy years living in New York City, I was lured to Providence by Lorne. Handsome as a television sitcom star, he also had an amused attitude and appreciation of me, the slightly distracted, head-in-the-clouds writer. To complete the picture, when Sam was three and I was pregnant with our daughter Grace, we rented a huge, slightly run-down Victorian house.

The house had thirteen rooms, three floors, and several staircases. Its poor insulation caused the curtains to blow about on windy days, even with the windows shut. The walls were painted pink or blue or purple with colorful scrolling trim. It had fireplaces that didn't work, soaring ceilings, and a bookcase that slid forward to reveal a secret door in Sam's room. In short, it was the house of my dreams.

The day Hillary knocked on the heavy bright green front door of my dream house, I was thirty-nine years old and seven months pregnant. I loved my husband. I had found happiness in motherhood and adored my son Sam. We had learned that this new baby was a girl, a girl who we would call Grace. Like Hillary on her wedding day seven years later, I saw only possibility ahead of me. I was hopeful and optimistic. I opened the door of my house, and Hillary walked in.

ON HER SECOND DAY with us, Sam told Hillary: "Hillary, I'm going to suck your toe."

Then he bent and did just that. He sucked her big toe.

Later, Hillary would tell us everything going through her mind in that instant: *I don't even know these people and I don't know what to do right now.* She confessed to us that she had been wearing her clogs all day, and her feet were sweaty.

"Hillary," Sam said, "you need to wash your feet."

But then he said, "Even so, I'd suck your toes again."

The night before her wedding, the fires still raging, the barbecue they'd planned was moved to an area considered safer than the original site. People were asked to come forward and give toasts. Sam was one of the first to do it. He told the story about sucking Hillary's toe. Everyone laughed at the audacity of his three-year-old self and the confidence in him still.

Sam turned to Hillary and said, "You get married tomorrow. I still have time before then." Then he said to her husband-to-be, "Watch out!"

I wanted to speak, to put into words what Hillary meant to me. Many words ran through my mind, but I couldn't speak. It wasn't just the smoke that caused the back of my throat to ache; it was the tears that I kept forcing back. At one point that night, I literally lost my voice. I could not speak.

From somewhere in the crowd, I heard a woman calling. "Grace! Gracie?" And then the delighted giggles of a little girl. Foolishly I ran toward that voice, that laughter. Everyone was wearing name tags, and I stumbled into a woman holding the hand of a little girl whose name tag said GRACE in big loopy letters.

The woman looked up at me, but I turned and walked away before she could say anything. In a tumble of memory, I remembered how Hillary's aunt had had a baby shortly after we'd had Grace, and that she had named that baby Grace. Here they were, mother and daughter. Grace. Gracie.

Quietly, I slipped away from the party, and back to our rented condo, the orange evacuation signs leading the way.

A WEEK AFTER Hillary moved in with us, I went into labor. She found me in our foyer, doubled over mid-contraction, waiting for Lorne to get the car. We hardly knew each other.

"Wow," she said, wide-eyed.

Two days later, I was home with Grace. Hillary's presence became immediately important. She had a soothing calm about her, a way of knowing what I needed before I even knew it.

That night, I awoke in horrible pain. *Funny,* I remember thinking, *I'm having an appendicitis attack right after having a baby.* But I soon realized that this was something else. At dawn I was in the emergency room where the doctor discovered a piece of placenta still left behind. He removed it and I was sent home, but by that afternoon my fever began to soar. Only Hillary was home with me, and she found me on the bathroom floor, wild with fever, scrawling my will on the back of a grocery receipt.

She called the doctor and got me antibiotics, then put me to bed, where I fell into a deep sleep. When I woke up, Hillary was sitting there with a toasted bagel topped with melted cheese. She brought Grace to me so I could breast-feed her.

"I'm right here," she said. The last words I heard before falling back to sleep.

MIRACULOUSLY, UNEXPECTEDLY, the fires changed course. Hillary's wedding day had blue skies, sunshine, that drop-dead stunning view. Lorne and Sam and I sat together, crying, as Hillary got married. We didn't have to tell each other what we were thinking. We all knew: *Grace should be here.* A line of little girls in colorful dresses led the wedding party, and I had to turn away from them to gaze out at the mountains beyond.

Later, from afar, I watched this other Gracie playing tag, eating strawberries, sitting on her mother's lap. I fought the urge to run from there, back to our condo with its new-wood smell and dangerously high deck. The stars hung heavily above us, and I looked up at them as if there really might be a heaven and Grace was looking down at Hillary's wedding. But I didn't really believe that, and my disappointment mingled with my grief.

I overheard some women saying that Hillary wanted to start a family right away. Immediately, they said. I remembered Hillary cradling my baby daughter, holding her on her lap, the hats she made for her and the way she would smash garbanzo beans for her lunch to be sure Grace had protein. Soon, I thought, Hillary would have a baby of her own, and she would bring all of her love and creativity to mothering her own child.

HILLARY USED TO make big salads for us at dinner.

She painted the dingy walls on the third floor warm colors with names like buttermilk and mink.

She gave us presents for our half birthdays.

On Saturday mornings she made waffles with warm maple syrup.

When my father was dying in the hospital, Hillary made pots of black bean soup and left me notes to find when I came home.

She put quotes from *Eloise* beside the telephone.

She planted pansies in our backyard.

She spent hours with Sam and Grace, teaching them to draw. Even Grace, a little over a year old, would hold a crayon and fill a blank paper with spirals. After Hillary graduated and moved away, Grace kept drawing. Grace wanted to go to RISD when she grew up. She took special art classes, and brought home projects that looked like someone much older had painted or drawn them. Grace moved slowly. She took her time. In the morning, as I tried to get Sam and Grace to school on time, Grace would still be looking for her shoes.

"Come on, Grace," I'd yell.

"You can't rush an artist, Mama," she'd tell me.

Hillary did that. She had made Grace an artist.

AFTER THE FLUSH of thank-you notes and wedding pictures, Hillary grew silent, adjusting to her new life. Back at home, we struggled to do the same. As time passed, our ache for Grace grew larger, more painful. I spent days sitting alone, simply missing her.

One night at dinnertime, our telephone rang.

"I'm pregnant!" Hillary told us. She was due in June. The baby was a boy. They had already picked out the name Henry.

We gushed together over the phone. Sam and

Lorne shouted their congratulations. After we hung up, we all sat back down at the table, silent. I thought of that red-haired girl at my door. Now she was an elegant and sophisticated woman. She was about to have a baby. Life was moving on, without Grace. As much as we had been forced to stand still, we couldn't really.

WHEN HILLARY CALLED to tell us that she was taking nine-month-old Henry to New York City to see Christo and Jeanne-Claude's Gates in Central Park, we decided to meet her there.

It had been three years since Grace had died. Slowly, we were back at work, out with friends again. Our loss still filled our home, every corner of it. It still filled us. Time doesn't heal, I had learned, it just keeps moving. And it takes us with it.

That blustery day in New York City, when Hillary stepped forward with her baby, she looked as if she had been a mother forever. To me, she had. In the easy way she placed him in the Snugli to making sure he ate the right foods at lunch, I saw her younger self taking care of my baby.

"I didn't fully get it," Hillary told us later that night. "I didn't really understand what losing Grace meant. Until I had Henry."

I nodded, remembering those wildfires at her wedding. I never actually saw them. I just knew they were out there. Once, I would have believed that of course they would stay away. I would have believed that danger could be averted.

CHAPTER SIX

Hold Me

I WRITE ABOUT how Hillary cared for Grace from the day she was born. And I write about Hillary's baby Henry. And I think about my babies. The first baby I ever held was my son Sam. I suppose over my lifetime babies had been put into my arms, but never newborns, and never for very long. Once I held Sam, however, I didn't want to put him down. Ever.

Despite the fact that he arrived at a meager four

and a half pounds, his skin the color of ripe boysenberries, in my arms he felt just right. "You have to put that baby down," my quartet of Italian aunts chided me. "You're going to spoil him." But I couldn't put him down. I felt as if I had been missing a body part for thirty-five years, and now, at last, I had found it. At night, after I tucked him into his crib, I felt weightless, unanchored. As soon as he woke hungry at dawn, I picked him up and brought him into bed with me so that I could hold him again.

I held Sam while I worked on my computer, when I cooked dinner, as I read the newspaper. Even when he was settled into the Snugli around my neck, I cradled him with my arms. I cannot say that holding Sam made me ecstatic, or superior, or even more maternal. I held him because my arms demanded it.

Before Sam was born, I was not a thirty-something woman with a loud or insistent biological clock. My arms happily held lovers, cats, friends; they held bouquets of flowers and bags overflowing with groceries. Sometimes my arms were completely free. Unencumbered, I walked the streets of my Manhattan neighborhood with twenty dollars in my pocket, no purse strings attached, my arms swinging in rhythm with the rest of me. At twice-weekly ballet classes, I learned to form my arms into perfect arcs for each position. "Pretend you are holding a big beach ball," my teacher commanded, and I held my empty arms in front of my chest, satisfied.

But after Sam was born, my arms were full. They opened wider to accommodate my growing son. When he was two, they ached a little if I carried him too long or too far. He wanted to be held less, preferring to run full speed around my apartment, to walk in his father's wing tips, to dance like mad to Beatles music. The less Sam needed my arms, the more they needed to be filled. *Perhaps,* I remember thinking, *this is how families grow.* A mother's need for her child snugged against her chest, for the musty smell of the top of a baby's head just beneath her own face, for the comforting weight of a baby in her arms.

I still remember the last time I held Sam in my arms. Of course there were many hugs to follow, many evenings with him on my lap and my arms around him. But the last time before he grew too big for me to comfortably hold him, when he could no longer rest on my hip as we took walks together. I was eight months pregnant with Grace. Sam was three. We went for our usual breakfast at a local café. Parking was tight that morning, so we had to park a good five or six blocks away. Sam scampered ahead of me, as he still does when we're out together. I shouted for him to stop at corners. To slow down. Waiting for me to catch up, he hopped from one foot to the other before racing away again.

On the way back to the car, a half a block from the café, Sam suddenly dropped to the ground and clutched his knee. "I can't move one more inch," he said dramatically. Way off in the distance, I saw the shiny silver roof of my car. "You have to," I told him. "I can't," he said, and began to cry. Awkwardly, I bent and picked him up. My pregnant belly kept me from holding him good and close as we made our slow trek to the car. Sweaty and out of breath, I buckled him into his car seat and said, "You're too big for Mommy to carry."

A few weeks later, Grace was born. When the

midwife placed her in my arms right after she was born, Grace looked right into my eyes with a steady, level gaze. She looked right into my heart at that moment. And it wasn't long before the Italian aunts were chastising me again. "Put that baby down!" But again, I refused.

A month after Grace was born, my father was diagnosed with lung cancer. He spent the next six months, before he ultimately died, in and out of hospitals. With Sam happily in nursery school, Grace and I spent our mornings with my father. I sat on the edge of his bed, holding Grace close. Dressed in pretty dresses with matching hats, Grace nestled in my arms and looked out at the world with that same steady gaze. Already, her eyes were the same light blue as my father's, and she would settle them on him and smile.

As an infant, Grace developed all kinds of respiratory problems. Coughing fits, pneumonia, raspy breathing, all plagued her. I would sleep holding her in the crook of my arm, her head resting on my shoulder. So that I literally held Grace day and night for the first year of her life. When she finally slept in her crib sometime after her first birthday, I didn't know where to put my arms without her in them. Although she snored through the nights, I struggled for sleep, first with my arms at my side, then with them bent at head level. Nothing worked. Until the early morning when she woke up, and I brought her back into bed with me, in my arms, and I could finally doze while she drank her first bottle of the day.

Sam came into bed too every morning. Often, I would have Grace resting in my right arm and Sam cuddling under my left arm. I would close my eyes and, like all mothers, revel in the sound of my children breathing beside me and the warmth of them in my arms.

Unlike her brother, Grace was content to sit on my lap and draw, or look at picture books. She did not leave my arms as she grew. Instead, she stayed close. After she finished eating dinner every night, she climbed onto my lap, wrapping her arms around me tight. I guess it is fair to say that when Sam was young, I held him in my arms; but Grace and I held each other.

April of 2002 arrived with unusually hot weather. By mid-month, Sam was already wearing shorts and Grace was putting on her new hot-pink-striped capri pants and sleeveless shirts. One day, after we dropped Sam off at school, as Grace and I walked across the parking lot to the car, I bent and swooped her up into my arms. At five years old, Grace was tall for her age, but slender, with long legs that she wrapped around my waist tightly, giggling that her mama could still pick her up and carry her. I can still vividly feel the tickle of her fine blonde hair against my cheek that morning and her perpetually sticky hands around my neck. Grace had worn glasses since she was two, and her wire-rimmed ones bounced against my own tortoiseshell glasses as we walked.

I can still feel the heft of my daughter in my arms that morning. I remembered carrying Sam those years before when I was pregnant, and felt grateful that Grace would probably let me hold her in my arms for some time to come.

It was the very next day, that strangely hot and humid April day, when Grace spiked that fever and I raced her to the emergency room. I have told all of this before. But somehow I need to say it again, to tell you that a doctor took my daughter from my arms, even as I struggled to hold on to her, looked me in the eyes, and said, "Your daughter is not going to make it."

They tried everything to save her, and they failed. We watched through a Plexiglas window, me pounding on it hard enough to bruise my elbows and palms, calling out my daughter's name. No mother should hold her dead child. But as I did, I could only remember how just two days earlier I had held her, warm and laughing, in my arms. How I had carried her to the car, breathing in Grace.

When we finally left the hospital, numb and stunned, we picked up Sam at our friends' house and told him the terrible news. That night, the three of us slept in one bed, holding each other until that cruel bright sun rose. Even then, I did not want to let Lorne or Sam go. I wanted to stay in that bed and hold them forever.

In those days and weeks after Grace died, I walked the house as if I might still find her there, my arms aching from wanting her in them. I found a trail of sparkles she had left after she had finished one of her art projects. I found her new hot-pink-striped capri pants in a happy heap on the floor, and her leopard rain boots resting against my own yellow ones. Her glasses were on my night table, left behind in our rush to the hospital. Her stuffed dog Biff and her blanket that she called Cow were all still tossed on the floor at the foot of my bed. These were the things I held in those horrible days. I lifted them to my nose and inhaled Grace's scent. I held them and cried.

I have read that when someone loses an arm or leg, for months afterward they still feel pain in their missing limb. A phantom limb, it is called, as if the outline or shadow of that limb is still there. That is what my arms became. Phantom limbs, aching for Grace. At night I would wake up in pain, my arms actually hurting with longing for her. It is hard to imagine that emptiness can cause pain, but my empty arms ached.

Sometimes, as months passed, I would find myself rubbing my arms hard, up and down, as if to bring them back to life, the way a person rubs their arms or legs when they "fall asleep." But my arms did not come back to life. The ache remained.

I tried to fill them. I learned to knit and held skeins of yarn in my arms. I held my dog, my books, my husband at night. But losing Grace made my arms emptier than they had ever been. Even now, as I write this, they tingle with pain. They reach out for what is gone. They have the kinetic memory of Grace, her soft five-year-old skin, her long legs, the tickle of her hair. I close my eyes. My arms are heavy. When I open them, I long for the steady gaze of her blue eyes looking back at me. They are the same blue as my father's.

But of course, when I open them, there is just the memory of Grace, the ache in my arms. Yesterday, Sam, now almost twelve years old, five feet six, so far from that four-and-a-half-pound baby I used to hold, came up behind me and picked me up. Like Fred Astaire lifting Ginger Rogers, he lifted me into his arms, ever so briefly. And in that instant I was in my son's arms, I remembered how briefly I was allowed to hold Grace. Then he put me down and walked off. I stood watching him go, my arms at my sides, my phantom limbs. Sam was opening his own arms wide, ready to hold whatever came his way.

That is what we all do, I suppose. We open our arms wide. We hold on. We hold on tight.

CHAPTER SEVEN

Staying

IT WASN'T ALWAYS this way. In fact, I leave things: dishes in the sink, clothes on the floor, magazines on tabletops, empty coffee cups in my car. I leave movies that are boring and parties that aren't fun. Once, in college, I left a waitressing job after an hour because they recycled the rolls from the breadbaskets. A few years later, in a bout of perpetual unemployment, I worked for thirty minutes in a travel agency before walking out. I leave the places I've called home with an ease and efficiency that is hard for some people to understand. In 1981, I rented the first floor of a renovated Victorian house in Marblehead, Massachusetts. A week before Christmas, I began to notice strange disappearances: the two sweet potatoes I left on the counter for that night's dinner, the silver icicles hanging from my Christmas tree, my springer spaniel Molly's kibble. One afternoon, staring at the missing pages of a paperback, a rat almost the size of Molly sauntered past me. The rat paused to check me out before continuing into the kitchen. I packed a suitcase and left, returning a month later only to salvage what the rats had left behind. Not only did I leave that apartment, I left Massachusetts for good.

It's probably no surprise that I also leave people. When I quit a job or moved away, I usually left the people who came with them: neighbors, coworkers, roommates. Sometimes I stayed in touch, but more often, either to put the bad stuff behind me or just eager to move into a new phase of my life, I simply left. When boyfriends got sullen, or disagreements grew too frequent, I broke up. Sure, I cried when "our" song came on the radio, called just to hear his voice on his answering machine, but that didn't stop me from walking out the next time a relationship hit some bumps.

There have even been a handful of times when I have left friendships I had thought would endure, not blithely but after feeling betrayed. I know that another kind of person, one who sticks things out, works on problems, has some character trait that I lack, would have fought to the bitter end to salvage even these relationships. That same type of person, I suppose, sends chatty Christmas cards to former neighbors and roommates; cries when she packs up her china to move; does her dishes and cleans her car; stays at the same job until she retires. Me? I leave.

The one place I thought for certain I would never leave was New York City. The first day I moved into my tiny sublet on Sullivan Street, in a former convent painted pink, I walked the maze of streets that made up my new neighborhood and actually felt the cells in my body shift and settle. Standing on the corner of Bleecker and Third that hot June day, I knew that I would be leaving jobs and lovers and even the apartment where I had just dropped a Hefty trash bag full of belongings, but I would not, ever, leave New York City.

A dozen years later, almost to the day, I was driving a rented U-Haul up the West Side Highway, watching my beloved city growing smaller in the rearview mirror. At thirty-five years old, I had fallen in love, hard and fast, and the man who was about to become my husband lived in Providence, Rhode Island. The night Lorne told me his plans for us—that I would move to Providence and live with him in a quaint historic house, that we would get married and have children and grow old together, I laughed and said, "I will never leave New York."

But I leave things. Even things I love. Even things I promise never to leave. So, with my cats screaming in their travel cases beside me and the truck bumping beneath me, with my future ahead of me, I left.

THE THING ABOUT MARRIAGE IS, you're not supposed to leave. You stand up in front of a hundred of your best friends and closest family members and promise them and the person you're marrying that you will stick it out. No matter what. I know people don't. All the time. I was even one of those people a couple years earlier, a person who left a marriage after five years. And having left one, the pressure to stay in the next one is even greater.

The thing about this marriage of mine was I wanted it to work. I really love my husband. He is handsome and kind and thoughtful and romantic and passionate and smart. Every year he makes my anniversary present out of our wedding picture, translated into paper or glass, whatever material tradition deems that year's gift is. It gives me real pleasure to watch the shelf where they sit gather more of these gifts—me clutching a bouquet of white tulips, both of us looking younger as time passes, our faces free of the pain and loss waiting for us just up ahead, those grins captured in tin and wood and cotton. I am happy to watch these accumulate, marking off another year together.

Still, for some time, I missed the life I had left behind. I missed walking down Bleecker Street before the city woke up, the quiet of Manhattan in the early morning, the smell of espresso and sugary pastries drifting from old Italian cafés; I missed the ballet class I took two mornings a week with its crazy array of NYU students, injured ballerinas, and plain old New Yorkers like me; I missed the noise from the street that played like a lullaby when I went to sleep at night; I missed the graduate students who crowded my apartment every Tuesday night for pasta and wine and discussions about writing fiction; I missed the friends I met for coffee, the friends I met for beer, the ones who fed my cats when I went out of town, and the ones who walked for hours with me on Sunday afternoons.

I missed all of it. I struggled to navigate the car through the strange and sudden one-way streets that littered my new city. I struggled to make friends. I wondered where a person bought good cheese here, where to find a movie theater that played foreign films, where the good independent bookstores were. I loved my husband, but every day when he put on his suit and walked out the door, I missed my real life, the one with lunches with magazine editors and book parties and other writers flopping on my sofa wondering if our new manuscripts would ever get finished.

I had promised my husband and all those people at my wedding that I wouldn't leave, but whenever we had a disagreement or a full-out fight, I imagined packing my bags and getting on Amtrak to Penn Station. Sometimes, I said it out loud: "I'm leaving! I'm going back to New York!" I imagined bundling up the kids and moving us all into an apartment not unlike the one I'd left in the West Village. But after a while my husband, who is calmer and more sensitive than I, pointed out that I had to stop threatening to do that. When you're married, he reminded me, leaving means divorce and emotional damage. He had no intention of leaving me, he said.

Both of us had parents who had stayed married to each other forever, and happily. Somehow they had worked out their differences. Was I really going to uproot my family and our lives because my husband liked to spend Saturdays cleaning instead of loafing? Or a dozen other reasons both small (how can he refuse the fruity olive oil I brought home so happily and drench his salad with bottled dressing?) and large (how could so many of his friends be so conservative?). The truth was, despite all of this, I had no intention of leaving him either. I just couldn't find my way in this new place, in my new life. Even after we had our son Sam, I struggled with the other mothers I met in their workout clothes and with their talk of home renovations. I didn't fit in here. That's what I felt. That's what I knew to be true. At night, when it was just my new little family, things seemed right. Eventually, we had our second baby, Grace, and Sam went off to a nursery school where I met women who were not unlike me. Some of them were also displaced New Yorkers. Some of them were writers.

Slowly, slowly, I began to make my way. I thought about leaving less. And when I did leave, to teach or give readings, I missed my family and home more. Arriving back at our little red colonial house after a week away, seeing Sam and Grace and Lorne waiting for me on the stoop with flowers in their hands, shouting, "Welcome home!" sweeping them into my arms, made me understand why people stick things out.

This is where I was three years ago: busy taking Sam and Grace to school, to ballet, to rehearsal for *Oliver!,* to playdates. They layered potatoes for potatoes au gratin and apples for apple crisp. They set the table together, deciding which color Fiestaware plate each of us should get: Sam always took purple and Grace always took pink and Lorne and I got whatever they decided for us. After dinner, we put on a bad dance tape and together we did the chicken dance and the Macarena and the Twist. At night, I read them Greek myths or Roald Dahl books. They fell asleep holding hands, and Lorne and I would stare down at our happy sleeping children. Then, on that hot April day, Grace spiked a fever and died thirty-six hours later from a virulent form of strep. She was five years old. Even now, I write these facts for the hundredth? thousandth? time and I cannot fully believe them. But they are true.

Some statistics say that fifty percent of couples who lose a child get divorced. Some statistics are even higher. It is easy to understand why. When your life is ripped apart, all the rules no longer apply. There is no order anymore: in your family, in your life, in the world. A week earlier, my mornings were all the same. I made my kids their lunches—ham on white bread, a yogurt, three cookies, and an apple for Sam; sliced cucumbers, cheese and crackers, blueberries for Grace—searched for clean underwear and matching socks, struggled to untangle Grace's hair and find Sam's homework, then drove them to school. Now, I didn't know what to do when I woke up. The life I had struggled so hard to create didn't exist anymore.

Eventually, Lorne went back to work. He put on his suit and went to his office. But my office was a tiny room off our dining room. It didn't provide an escape for me. My work was a blank page that needed filling. But I couldn't think or form sentences. Suddenly, the woman who ran away when things got tough had nowhere to escape. Our house filled with my friends. They held my hand and did our laundry and picked Sam up from school. They climbed into bed with me if they had to. In the evening, when Lorne returned from work, he came home to a house full of people.

These are the kinds of things that tear grief-stricken couples apart. I craved noise and conversation; he needed solitude. Lorne took comfort in sitting at Grace's grave and talking to her; I hated going there, hated the idea that my little girl was there, and avoided it. Church became a refuge for

Lorne; but I hated God. The different ways two people grieve are enough to make them seem like strangers to each other. But losing Grace did the opposite for me. I saw the man I married as more precious.

On a New Year's Eve six years earlier, we conceived Grace together. Except for the midwife, we were the only two people there when she was born. He's the one who put on the Simon and Garfunkel CDs, and sat with me in the whirlpool until we climbed onto the king-size bed and, with me pushing and Lorne coaching, brought Grace into the world. My husband is the person who, when Grace's head emerged, said, "Here she is! She's the most beautiful baby in the world." He cut her umbilical cord and walked with the midwife across the room and weighed our baby daughter. Together, we held her and said her beautiful name over and over, whispering it to her, announcing her to the world.

Lorne and I were by her side five short years later, in a cold room in an intensive care unit at the children's hospital, whispering her name again, this time desperately trying to keep her from leaving us.

I watched my husband climb onto the hospital bed, amid tubes and machines and monitors, press his lips to our dying daughter, and sing her the Beatles' "Love Me Do." We stood together, banished from her room, pounding on a Plexiglas window as they tried, one more futile time, to save her life. We pounded on that window and together yelled her name: "Grace! Grace!" We did those things.

We have been crying in each other's arms ever since. At first, after friends went home to their own families, we fell into bed together, exhausted and so filled with grief that we could only cry; words were too difficult, too meager. But slowly, our crying framed our stories. "Rerember?" we would ask each other, using Grace's mispronunciation of "remember." Rerember the night she was born? The way she used to crawl, dragging one leg behind her? Rerember when she stuck the goldfish cracker up her nose? When she wouldn't leave the stage after she danced in a ballet of *The Polar Express* but instead stayed there, bowing and bowing, alone in her white tulle?

These memories are ours, Lorne's and mine. We are the only people in the world who hold Grace's history. I used to think that leaving was the thing to do when times were hard. But having now lived through the hardest time, having made it because Lorne was by my side, holding me, and I was there holding him, I understand the virtue, the necessity, of staying.

I am writing this on the eve of my eleventh wedding anniversary. Tomorrow night, Lorne will give me a gift. It will be our wedding picture cast in some new material. I am holding a bouquet of white tulips; we are both grinning out at the world, our faces hopeful and happy; we are facing the future arm in arm.

CHAPTER EIGHT

Hello, God! It's Me, Ann

WHEN I MET my husband-to-be, Lorne, I used to walk every Saturday morning from my apartment in the West Village in New York City, up Hudson Street, to St. Luke's church where I helped cook meals for people with AIDS. This was in 1992, and my neighborhood, where Christopher Street with its condom shops and gay bars with blackened windows, was especially ravaged by the disease. It was common to see young men whose faces had splotches of red and purple, leaning heavily on canes or walkers as they made their slow way down the block.

I never actually set foot in that church. Instead, I walked through a gate, past a garden that bloomed bright in warm weather, and into the kitchen. There, I chopped and sautéed, diced and sweated, rolled and pounded, preparing the high-fat, high-caloric food prescribed by doctors. I am Italian-American, raised with the philosophy that feeding people nourishes their souls as well as their stomachs. Someone else plated those potatoes au gratin and crème brûlées; someone else sliced the leg of lamb marinated in yogurt and spices; someone else set the tables and served the food and cleaned up afterward. Me, I cooked. And by cooking those few hours, I nourished my own soul as well.

By this time in my life, I had dabbled in and explored just about everything. When I ruptured my Achilles tendon hiking when I was twenty-two, I wrote "Buddhist" on the emergency room form under religion. I puzzled over the silence and simplicity of Quaker meetings in a meetinghouse in the Berkshires one long lonely winter there. I lit seder candles and ate challah on Friday nights during a relationship with a Jewish man, and visited the Ethical Culture Society down the street from my apartment in Brooklyn. I read everyone from Saint Augustine to Lao Tzu to the Bagwhan Rashneesh, and finally, at the age of thirty-five, newly divorced, moderately successful, my spirituality felt rich and large and comfortable.

In many ways, by the time I met Lorne, I had come full circle. My family's spirituality came from people—helping them, sharing with them, talking to them, and, yes, feeding them. I grew up sitting around a kitchen table with a platter of spaghetti and meatballs in the center, a pot of coffee bubbling on the stove, and various generations of aunts, uncles, cousins, and friends filling every chair and corner of the room. At that table, I learned about love and loss, faraway places and broken hearts, strange diseases and miracle cures. As one of the youngest, I didn't say very much. I ate wine biscuits twisted into pretzel shapes and hard bread dipped into tomato sauce, tight batons of prosciutto and crunchy stalks of fennel dripping with olive oil. I ate and I listened and my soul and heart grew and expanded in that kitchen.

Ostensibly we were Catholic. But on snowy Sundays, or busy Sundays, or sometimes on any old Sunday, my grandmother climbed onto our kitchen table, threw holy water at us, and gave us special dispensation to stay home from church. Instead, I helped her mix the meat and spices for meatballs, and got to eat them hot from the frying pan. In summer, we abandoned church altogether and spent Sundays from sunrise until dusk at a lake an hour from home. There, in the cold early morning, my father fried bacon and eggs in a wrought-iron skillet over an open fire. My cousins and I chased each other across the pine-needled floor of the woods, ran in and out of the water, played Frisbee and frozen tag, while our parents fed us sandwiches of deviled ham or salami and provolone. When it got dark, we huddled together at campfires after dinners of barbecue chicken and marinated London broil, and toasted marshmallows on the long branches we had collected during the late afternoon.

When I was twelve, I abandoned Catholicism and churchgoing after the priest told me during confession that my entire family was going to hell because we spent summer Sundays together at the beach instead of attending mass. Even then I understood that my spirituality came more from those long days swimming, hiking, and eating together than it did from sitting bored in an overheated church.

Although our mutual lapsed Catholicism was one of the things we shared stories about when we first met, Lorne had in fact been a more serious Catholic than I ever was. Various family members sang in the choir, and the kids all joined the youth group, playing guitars and taking ski trips and camping trips. While my parents looked relieved when I announced I was finished with church, Lorne continued attending mass all the way through college and into adulthood.

I realized right away that Lorne was more religious than I. When his earlier marriage was falling apart, he had gone to talk to his minister; when mine was on the rocks, I sought solace with friends and family. I didn't *have* a minister, of course. But Lorne did. He attended a big ornate Congregational church in Providence, where he joined various committees and ate at potluck suppers. When he drove, he got inspiration from tapes of famous sermons by renowned preachers. One summer, years earlier, when he was in graduate school, he worked for Church World Service, and still counted the various ministers and Riverside Church administrators among his best friends. It seemed to me that church and spirituality were linked in Lorne's world, and separated in mine.

But when we fell in love that spring, it was fast and furious. The power and passion of that love made me believe that we could overcome everything: ex-spouses, political differences, the two hundred miles that lay between us. Spirituality—a private thing—and religious alliances and alienations seemed easier to work with than all of the other obstacles in our path. Besides, when kissing someone makes you swoon, makes your mind go blank, makes your stomach tumble, it feels at that moment like nothing else really matters.

That was why, in what felt like a minute, I had left my beloved New York City behind to be with Lorne in Providence. Pregnant with our first child Sam, I became a recalcitrant, though not entirely unhappy, member of that Congregational church. By the time I'd had our second baby, Grace, I was almost enjoying the social aspects the church offered. At the coffee hours and auctions and sing-alongs, I would spot another mom from Sam's pre-school, or the parents of a baby Grace's age. Taken out of my familiar single, childless world of Manhattan, I was having to find new friends, new places to meet people, a new way of life. Church became one more way to navigate this new territory of wife and mother, one more connection in a marriage already solidly passionate and intimate.

Although sometimes I left church spiritually invigorated or intellectually challenged, more often I left simply happy to have watched Sam lead Grace hand in hand to children's hour, or delighted at the sight of them in makeshift costumes during the Christmas pageant. Even now, I can muster something like that spiritual bliss I felt back then when I imagine this tableau: my family—Lorne, Sam, Grace, and me—dressed in our Sunday best, Sam's shirt untucked, Grace's hair snarled, my hand tucked into my husband's, our bellies full of home-made waffles, the four of us entering that big yellow church with the sun streaming through its elaborate Tiffany windows.

Then, the unthinkable happened. The life I had so carefully nurtured for a decade came to a grinding, confusing halt. Who does a mother turn to for blame and hate at a time like this? God, of course. For all the uncountable moments over these past ten years when I had paused to thank God, now I turned on Him. Just a few days before Grace died, I had dropped her off at her kindergarten one sunny morning. It was uncharacteristically warm for April, and I swear the sunlight pouring from that bright blue sky looked positively golden spilling onto my station wagon as I watched Grace walk inside, her purple-spotted backpack bouncing behind her. The sight of her, and all that sunshine, made me so grateful that I was overcome with emotion. I pulled over, and thanked God for this day and these beautiful children.

When Grace died a few days later, my betrayal was enormous. I told this story to our minister, a woman with two young children of her own. "It's so terrible," she kept saying over and over. But had I drawn attention to our good fortune that day in my car? Had I jinxed my family? I had read somewhere that Hmong babies wear elaborate hats that look like flowers from above so that spirits flying past will mistake them for blossoms and leave them alone. Had my gratitude somehow tempted fate? But the minister could only shake her head and tell me how terribly sad it all was. Please, I told my friends who stood sentry by my door and telephones, please don't make me talk to her again.

Foolishly, I believed that clergypeople might hold the answers I screamed to God for every night. I watched as my husband's seemingly unshakable faith wobbled too. Together, a unified force, we drove to talk to famous rabbis, priests, religious experts on loss. Dutifully, Lorne took notes, asked questions, listened. But I saw how their eyes drifted toward the clocks on their office walls, and when an hour passed, they assured us time would heal and sent us on our miserable way.

Still, Lorne took solace in these visits in a way that I could not. The only shard of comfort I could find was in friends' willingness to sit with me for endless hours and let me wail at God and the world. Lorne believed in a randomness in the world that I did not; I sought answers where he believed there were none. Even in our grief, we made room for each other's spiritual differences. People fed us with aluminum pans of lasagna and fancy stuffed chicken and thick, creamy soups; chocolate chip cookies and brownies; expensive wine and single malt whiskey. But at night, in our three-legged house, we found comfort, as we always had, in each other's arms. Despite the long hours apart—Lorne at his office, me at home with friends—in our bed alone our old passion helped us get through until morning. More often than not, crying became part of our lovemaking. Our bed, where Sam and Grace so happily tumbled into each morning, where we all had squeezed together to watch movies, now held our grief and our fragile selves together. So that even as our loss brought renewed spiritual disagreements, that passion that had brought us together remained, amazingly, unchanged.

That summer, I taught writing at the Chautauqua Institute in upstate New York. The minister there gave a series of morning sermons on the landscape of grief. His own wife had died young, and that loss sent him on a spiritual journey away from the familiar church and city he had known. Changing from minister to teacher, moving from

Nashville to Indianapolis, traveling to far-flung places, had all been part of his journey of grief. When the sermon ended, I made an appointment to talk with him.

That afternoon, in the hot study of the Victorian house where he was staying, I told him about losing Grace. I told him how ministers and priests and rabbis had only been able to offer platitudes, instead of answers, or even comfort. Then I said out loud the horrible thing I had been thinking for months now. "I don't believe in God anymore," I said. Dan nodded. He understood. It's difficult to believe in something that doesn't make sense anymore, he told me.

When he stood, I realized my hour was up. Although I knew he wouldn't make hollow promises about time healing as he ushered me to the door, I still felt the familiar anger rising in me. Who had taught these religious people, I wondered, that a mother's heart could be healed in sixty minutes. But Dan surprised me. "Well," he said, "you're stuck with me now. Here's my e-mail address, my home phone, my cell phone. Contact me anytime. Day or night."

Surprised and grateful, I left that room feeling spiritually validated. I could hate God. I could not believe in Him at all. Why should I put myself through the motions of going to church when I felt betrayed by it? There were so many things I had stopped doing to avoid the horrible pain they brought. I never drove down the tree-lined street where Grace's school sat or the block behind Brown University where she took ballet class. When I passed the Children's Hospital where she died, I kept my eyes focused on the highway ahead, never glancing to my right. I didn't go to Old Navy or open the Hanna Andersson catalogues that seemed to slide through my mail slot with an alarming frequency. If I could avoid all of this, then why should I go to church ever again?

No sooner had that first autumn with Grace arrived with its onslaught of back-to-school clothes and lunch boxes and promise than Grace's birthday came. I drank too much rosé and ate her favorite foods of sliced cucumbers and shells with butter and parmesan. Birthdays, back to school, and the horrible promise of Thanksgiving and Christmas right around the corner. How was I going to get through it all?

Then, one Sunday morning, Lorne said he wanted us all to go to church. I wanted to flat out refuse. But so desperate was I for help, so desperate to make our little broken family whole again, that I went despite my discomfort. As we slid into our usual pew, a family of three now instead of four, I felt everyone's pity pouring over us. It wasn't pity that I wanted, or even sympathy. I wanted Grace back. And short of that, I wanted God or someone to help me understand why she was gone and what to do without her. Sam squeezed my hand. "I want to go home," he whispered. I glanced at him and saw his cheeks were wet with tears. When it was time for children's hour, I watched as all the same pairs and trios of siblings skipped down the aisles together, hair ribbons dangling, shoelaces untied. Sam was weeping now, unable to control himself. We all were. The minister's words about kindness and fellowship sounded hollow. I couldn't wait to get out of there. I never wanted to go back.

But Lorne, in that openhearted way of his, found solace in the sympathy of the congregation and comfort in the minister's sermon. All those years ago, our different and varying views on spirituality had seemed interesting and manageable. Now we stood on opposite sides of a spiritual divide. Lorne still believed in the Christian tenets that had helped him through his lifetime; I once again found myself questioning them, unbelieving, alone. We debated our different opinions and needs until, with no truce in sight, we turned silent.

Over the next months, I vacillated between gritting my teeth and accompanying Lorne to church, where I often walked out over some philosophical disagreement or simple frustration with the banality of the service, and digging in my heels and refusing to go. "It makes me too sad," I explained. "It makes me sad too," Lorne said. Still, somehow being there did help him in his grief and only made me angrier. On the mornings I stayed behind, I drove the fifteen miles to my mother's house and let her make me a big breakfast of bacon and eggs and toast and coffee. I found much more comfort in an hour there than I did at church.

I remembered how during my years of visiting different religious places, I had enjoyed the Sunday mornings I spent at a Unitarian church. When I'd first moved to Providence, I had gone alone to one right up the street from our house, and found it more appealing than the Congregational church we attended. But Lorne preferred ours, and didn't like that Unitarians weren't Christians. Since it mattered more to him than it did to me, I let it go. But now I wondered if some spiritual compromise was necessary. We made an appointment to meet with the minister of our church to see if she had any ideas about our spiritual differences.

In her high-ceilinged office, she told us about other married congregants who didn't come to church together. Some went to separate churches. Others had one spouse who didn't go to church at all. I tried explaining how church—this church, in particular—made me feel. How seeing children Grace's age there opened my grief all over again; how the shadow of her in the pageant, emerging from church school, holding Sam's hand on the way to children's hour, all of it, made me want to run out of there screaming. "It sounds like you shouldn't come then," she said, and although her advice held both logic and compassion, I once again felt let down. Ultimately, my spirituality was between me and me. Yet I felt torn in different directions.

Shouldn't someone in charge help me straighten these feelings out?

Together in that office, we came up with a plan to try other churches. Since we only went to church a couple of times a month anyway, this left me with only one Sunday to have to face my demons here. The next week, we all went to a Baptist church with an African-American congregation. The minister's sermon was powerful, and the experience satisfying. Then the holidays came, I left for teaching out of town, we went away, and before I knew it we were back to the old Sunday struggle, our decision to visit other places once a month abandoned. In some ways, I dropped the ball on finding these alternative religious experiences. Grief had worn me down; it had exhausted me. My desire to read the religion section of the newspaper to find interesting sermons, unusual services, different congregations, flagged. Deep down I knew this idea was just a stalling technique. I wasn't going to join the alternative church that met in a real church's basement; I wasn't going to return to my Catholic roots; I didn't want to become Episcopalian, Zen Buddhist, or a practitioner of TM. I just wanted to be angry at God.

I began to wonder what I would do had I been my younger self, instead of this forty-seven-year-old woman. When I was in a relationship with a practicing Jew, I had given him free reign: no Christmas tree, no Easter eggs. Instead, his contemporary silver crafted menorah held center stage on our shelf of treasures. Although it could be argued that my own beliefs were subjugated to his, an error women far away from middle age often make, in truth I felt comfortable enough with my spirituality to keep it to myself. I spent Christmas and Easter with my family, and he came along, happily imbibing our homemade sangria and Christmas gifts. It was almost a relief not to drag a Christmas tree up to our fourth-floor walk-up. Since my own family didn't attend church, I never felt that I gave up that much.

But now I had a child to consider, a broken heart, a churchgoing husband, and I didn't believe in God. In many things, middle age has allowed me to easily admit defeat. I no longer feel like I have to do a difficult hike because everyone else is doing it, or that I must keep up shallow friendships, or that I have to read a book I don't like all the way to the end. That same maturity that has allowed me to prioritize all kinds of things now made me more confused. In a moment of clarity, I agreed to go back to church.

It was another September, and I harbored a small hope that I would find strength in church that Sunday to face what had slayed me last year: back to school and Grace's birthday. I felt good seeing how this simple decision to go with him without an argument made my husband so happy. What was two hours a month after what we had been through?

We settled into our pew, and as the choir began to raise their voices, I skimmed the program. As an overachiever, I always like to know ahead of time what the Bible verses are going to be so I can read them before they're read out loud, and I like to mark the hymns that are going to be sung. That was when I saw that coming up, soon, was "Amazing Grace." When you have named your daughter Grace and she is alive and thriving, it is exciting to see her name in books as the snappy protagonist or on the sides of pharmaceuticals, and even in this most beautiful hymn. But everyone in that church, including the people who chose that song, knew two things: Grace's birthday was that week, and that song had been sung at her funeral, achingly beautifully, by my sister-in-law.

Already prayers had been spoken and other songs had been sung. At any moment the organ would play those heartbreaking opening chords. I grabbed my coat and walked out of the pew, down that center aisle, and out the door, where I sat on a cold stone bench and cried like I might never stop. When I felt an arm slip around my shoulders, I expected it to be one of the ministers or other laypeople who help out during the service. But it was my stalwart friend Amy, who had sat and held my hand, took me out for teary dinners, taught me how to cast off when I learned to knit in those dark new days of grieving.

"I saw what was on that program and I couldn't believe it," Amy said. "Then I saw you walk out."

Amy sat with me in the sharp autumn sun, and let me cry and rant against church and God, while Lorne remained inside. I wondered how he could do it, how he could sit there and let that song wash over him. Was he stronger than I? Or was this just another example of our different ways through grief?

We made another meeting with our ministers. "How could you?" I asked them. "You knew how hard it is for me to walk in here, and then you play that song." I explained that as a popular and beautiful hymn, it should be played. But so close to Grace's birthday? And without any warning? Even if that didn't occur to anyone, we were always getting calls to come to meetings or to ask us to bake cookies or work on a Sandwich Brigade for the homeless shelter, but no one could call us to apologize after they saw me walk out in tears?

It *was* a mistake. They were sorry. It would never happen again. In fact, they would not play "Amazing Grace" in September, or in April, the month Grace died. I looked into the face of these people—people no closer to God than I was—and saw their fear. Both of them had young children. If I had lost Grace, anything could happen. Was that why it was so difficult for them to offer comfort, to help me come up with answers, to massage my wounded spirituality?

In the gumbo of spirituality, of church and religion and God and beliefs and faith, it is hard to separate one from the other. It has been three years since Grace died. My husband has turned fifty since then. He is a handsome man, but sorrow has taken some of the twinkle from his eyes. He is a man who believes in the power of church and religion. He wants a simple thing: for his wife and his son to stand beside him and lift their voices in a song of gratitude for what we have and for having had Grace at all. I try to give him this. It isn't easy, but I am trying.

I see now that my own journey has led me back to what I knew as a child facing down a priest hidden by the screen of the confessional; what I knew as a younger woman living alone in New York City, chopping basil and peeling potatoes for the dying men in my neighborhood.

It took two years from that summer day when I boiled water for pasta again and cooked dinner for my family until I once again began to cook for them every evening. I spend too much money on a perfectly ripe cheese. I buy fancy crackers from Italy. I boil the water for spaghetti, and carefully cook pancetta and garlic to make a carbonara. I toss this with the pasta, mix in eggs and good parmesan. Right before I serve it, I add two egg yolks. This is the secret to real spaghetti carbonara. I believe in this: good food, the sounds of forks against plates, the perfect blend of flavors. And later, in the night, I believe in the quiet sound of my son's deep breathing as he sleeps; I believe in my husband's hand, resting even in sleep on my breast, trusting, loving, there. Even now, there are still days so beautiful, I almost believe in God.

CHAPTER NINE

There

TIME DOESN'T HEAL. It just passes. One day we rearrange the family room, moving the couch so it faces this way, buying a stand for the television. One day we decide to paint the living room green. We turn a spare room into a knitting room to hold all of my yarn. Sam buys me an *Oxford English Dictionary* for my birthday; it is the thing I have most wanted for all of my adult life and now it sits on an old library dictionary stand, stately and wise.

I sell my station wagon and buy a bright orange VW Bug convertible. I grow my hair long. Sam stands at five feet eleven. I put turquoise Marimekko sheets on our bed. Sam's bunk beds are gone, replaced with a double bed. Time passes and I look around and see how many things have changed since Grace died.

Now her shoes stand like sentries at the top of the stairs. Four pairs: leopard rain boots, sparkly red Mary Janes, blue Skechers sneakers, worn metallic pink slip-ons. They break my heart, those shoes. I cannot go up or down the stairs without seeing them, which is why we put them there. They are lined up, toes pointed out, ready to be put on, ready to skip down those stairs, out the door, into the world.

Sometimes, I cannot go down the stairs without touching one of them, like a talisman. Sometimes, I find a dust bunny wrapped around a shoe, catching on the glitter or trapped under a Velcro strap. That makes me stop to clean that entire corner. If there's dust, we are reminded that no one wears those shoes anymore. We are reminded that our funny blonde Grace is dead.

"I hope," a man told me at dinner one night about a year after Grace died, "that you've cleaned out her room."

We were sitting in a fancy Italian restaurant, eating homemade gnocchi and drinking Pinot Grigio. The man's wife had died some years back, and like many people who had lost a loved one, he was trying to help us, to show us that we would survive. *Here I am,* these people seemed to say. *Look! I made it!* I didn't doubt that at some distant point in the future, I would still be alive, still enjoying a good glass of wine and good food. What I wasn't sure of was *how* I was going to get to that place without Grace.

"Nothing worse than a shrine," the man said.

The truth is, before Grace died, in fact, for my entire life, I've loved visiting shrines of all kinds. Homemade ones, official ones, religious ones, personal ones. I used to love to travel to offbeat locations in foreign cities to find shrines to dead cats, to victims of war, to small-town heroes.

"Get rid of her clothes," the man said. "Make the room a guest room or something."

GRACE WALKED OUT of her room one day a healthy, vibrant five-year-old and never walked back in. Her ballet tights smelling of her stinky feet lay in a tangle on the floor. A basket beside her bureau held all of her socks—the leopard print and zebra print, the ones covered with pink hearts, the crazy stripes, and polka dots. On a shelf in her closet sat a pink bag. In it, I had put a *New York Times* from September 24, 1996, the day she was born; her sonogram pictures; the tiny newborn hat she had worn in the hospital; dozens of little things that celebrated the day she was born. I had imagined doing something clever with them when she turned sixteen, or went off to college, or got married. Now I cannot bear to open that bag with all of its ignorant joy.

The funny thing is Grace never slept in her bedroom. Once she left her crib behind, my mother and I went to a local furniture store and bought an antique white bedroom set. A sleigh bed and bookshelf and a bureau with a scrolled mirror. Her cousin bought her sheets covered with cats. My friend handed down a comforter from France. We kept the green rocking chair that I rescued from a beach in Far Rockaway, New York, long before

Grace or Sam was born; that was the chair I used to nurse in when she was a baby, the chair I rocked her to sleep in each night.

Grace loved her room, and often went in there to paint on the easel that sat in one corner, or to change her outfit, or to get a book. But she slept in Sam's room—Sam on the top bunk, Grace on the bottom. Sam got a thrill out of threatening her. "Next year you have to sleep in your room," he'd say. But she didn't believe it for a minute. She knew he needed her there as much as she wanted to be there. Grace loved to sleep. As a baby, she slept through the night early and easily. She liked to sleep late whenever she could. But Sam hated naps and bedtime. He feared the shadows that trees sent spilling across the walls at night, feared robbers roamed our yard. "How do you fall asleep so fast?" he'd ask Grace, and she would put her hands behind her head, close her eyes, mutter, "Like this, Sam," and go to sleep. At night, when bad dreams woke Sam, or kept him from falling asleep at all, he climbed into the bottom bunk with Grace. He would wake her up, and the two of them would talk in the dark until, sleepy, he could finally go back up, and fall asleep.

It would be easy, then, to think of Grace's room as a storeroom, a playroom, a room easy to clean out. But like the entire house, like each of our hearts and minds, Grace's fingerprints were everywhere. Grace was the kid who, when playing the game "I went on a trip and in my trunk I packed . . ." said *rambutan* for the letter *r*. Grace was the kid who started wearing glasses when she was only two. "The thing about kids this little," the ophthalmologist warned us, "they won't wear their glasses. They pull them off, lose them, forget them, break them." Not Grace. She loved her glasses, and from the minute she got her first pair of wire-rimmed ones she wore them. When I told her what the doctor had said, she rolled her eyes. "Why wouldn't I wear them?" she asked me. "I can't *see* without them." Grace painted and drew and colored all the time, everywhere. Papers filled with a special swirl she used to make still show up around the house. And there, right on that antique white bureau, is her name, written in her own hand with a red crayon.

The first time I walked into Grace's room after she died, when the reality of what had happened to us in the past forty-eight hours was still unbelievable, the first things I saw were those tights. I saw them and I screamed, not the kind of scream that comes from fright, but the kind that comes from the deepest grief imaginable. It is a scream that comes when there are no words to express what you feel. It is an argument with God or life or death. It is a scream that rails against logic and fate and everything there is. I saw those tights. I screamed. I closed the door to the room, hard. Then I sat on the floor in the hallway outside Grace's room and I cried.

My friend Sharon came to me every day. She did simple things and she did enormous things. One of those things was going into our basement and doing the laundry I had begun the day Grace got sick and died. Our house was built in 1792, and our basement is of the creepy, stone-floor variety. The ceilings are low. The pipes are wrapped with something to keep the asbestos from killing us. The furnace makes scary noises. There are mice down there. And mousetraps. Still, I used to find a kind of pleasure in venturing into that basement and doing the laundry. I liked separating our clothes into piles—Grace's, Sam's, Lorne's, mine. Grace's purple and pink pants and skirts mingling with Sam's bright orange T-shirts; her little underwear decorated with Disney princesses tangled up with Sam's miniature boxers, Lorne's extra large ones. I liked the smell the Tide with bleach alternative left behind, the warmth of the clothes when they came out of the dryer.

But Grace's death left everything in mid-cycle. I would never go down to that basement and finish what I had begun on that warm April afternoon when my life stretched before me in endless loads of ever-growing laundry. So Sharon went down and finished the wash cycles. She put everything in the dryer. She folded Grace's underwear and shirts and skirts and pajamas. She cried while she did this, but she got it done. Then she put Sam's clothes in his drawers, and Lorne's and my clothes in our room, and then she went into Grace's room and carefully placed her clean clothes on the bed she never slept in.

AS MONTHS PASSED, I would sometimes dare myself to push open that door and go into that room. I would stand in that doorway and see Grace's crayoned name on her bureau, see that pile of clean laundry on her bed, see her easel, her tutus. See everything but Grace. And I would pull the door shut and run.

Most of our house was built in 1792, but thirty or so years ago the owners put on an addition, an L-shaped thing that gives us a big kitchen and full bathroom downstairs and two bedrooms and a third full bathroom upstairs. The extension, unlike the rest of the house, which is heated by that noisy furnace in the basement, has a bad electrical heating system. One of those upstairs bedrooms belongs to my stepdaughter Ariane. The other bedroom is Grace's.

For that first winter, we didn't turn on the upstairs heat for those rooms at all. Now that she is a teenager, Ariane doesn't visit as often. Both of the bedrooms stayed empty that winter. One afternoon in the dead of winter, I opened the door to Grace's room and it was freezing cold in there. I stepped in, sat on the floor, and touched her socks—so small, those socks—every pair in that basket. I could see my breath in that room. I opened one of the drawers in her bookshelf and looked through her sketch pad. Pages filled with her swirls. Pages of her practicing writing her name. Sometimes she wrote Sam's too. On one page she'd written a list of names of people who could join a club she and Sam were planning. On one page she'd written: *I love you, Mommy! Love, Grace.*

SOMEONE SENDS US a brochure about a woman who takes dead people's clothes and makes teddy bears out of them.

Someone calls and gently tells us that our church is having a clothing drive for a homeless shelter.

Someone offers to make a quilt out of Grace's clothes for us.

Someone offers to go in there and pack everything away. They promise not to get rid of a thing. They will just put everything in boxes and label those boxes and put them in our creepy basement.

I tell Lorne that I can't do any of it. "You don't have to," he says. So we leave it all untouched.

IN OUR MUDROOM by the side door we have hooks for coats and shelves for shoes and boots and more shelves for hats and mittens and scarves. On the morning of the day before Grace died, I was struggling to get the kids out the door for school. Grace was slow. Slow to wake up. Slow to eat her breakfast. Slow to get dressed. She still needed me to put on her socks, to brush her hair, to button or zip or snap. She was only five years old.

That morning we were running late and Sam was saying, "Hurry up!" and I was saying, "Come on, Grace!" and Grace smiled at us and said, "You can't hurry an artist, guys." Sam got in the car and was holding the door open for Grace and as she walked through the mudroom something caught her eye. She bent and tugged and pulled out her favorite winter hat. Multicolored stripes, it came to two big points on top of her head and each point had a pom-pom on it that bounced whenever she moved. "Look! My pom-pom hat!" Grace said, excited, and she pulled it on her head. "It's too hot for that today," I said, "but I'm glad you found it." I pulled it off as she walked past me to the car. Her hair flew with static electricity. I hung the pom-pom hat on one of the coat hooks, right above her pale blue winter coat, the one that matched her eyes.

It wasn't just Grace's room. It was the pom-pom hat and the pale blue coat and the pink fleece pullover and the fucshia button-down sweater, all of them hanging on those hooks in the mudroom. After she died, I would bury my face in that jacket, that sweater, and I would breathe deeply, as if I really could capture some small part of her still.

UNEXPECTEDLY, A DAY ARRIVES. Three years have passed. It is an ordinary Saturday in February and I know I can do it. I can go into Grace's room and I can put away her things. I come up with a system. Plastic bins for those things too precious to give away. Masking tape and Sharpies to label them. Boxes for those things to donate to the homeless shelter. Trash bags. I used to go into Grace's and Sam's rooms with the same supplies each season. Snowsuits and boots. Bathing suits and flip-flops. Everything organized and labeled so I could easily find it the next summer, the next winter. I used to write in big letters: *Grace, age 3, summer. Grace, age 5, winter.* That is where those boxes stopped.

Now I enter her room and I do not pause to think about anything except getting the task done. I begin with that laundry, still folded and lying right where Sharon left it. I shove the underwear into trash bags. I hold up the other items, one by one, and I begin to cry. If the item is something that immediately reminds me of Grace, if it was one of her favorites, if we have a picture of her in it, I place it in a plastic bin. If not—a plain yellow T-shirt, a pair of pants I don't even remember, I put it in a box to give away.

I cry.

I move to her bureau. There is her name in red crayon. I open each drawer and pull out shirts and shorts and dresses and capri pants and jeans. Everything, everything is Grace. I am surrounded by Grace's things, but Grace is gone. This idea fills me until I think I cannot breathe anymore. I am crying so hard that I have to keep my glasses off because they are so tear-streaked. Sam stands in the doorway, bouncing from one foot to the other nervously.

"Can I help?" he says, my brave eleven-year-old son.

I shake my head. "I'm fine," I say.

"It's okay," I say when he still doesn't leave.

He runs down the hall, fast.

The bags, the boxes, the bins are all filling up as the room empties. The closet yields more surprises, more pain, more memories. Here is a coat I bought on sale at a fancy store in New York City. Thick hot pink corduroy with a paisley-print collar, I bought it in the only size left: 6. *She'll wear it eventually,* I thought. But she never got to be a size 6, and here is that coat with the tags still hanging from it, waiting for her to grow up.

I cry.

Here is the pink bag I filled with the *New York Times* from the day she was born, her sonogram pictures, the hat she wore in the hospital as a newborn.

Here is the bathing suit she picked out the week before she died. A lime one-piece with big red and blue circles all over it. Tags still on. That summer after she died, I was sitting on the beach and a little girl in this same suit ran past me. I wanted to throw sand at her. I wanted to rip that bathing suit off her. But I just gathered my things and left the beach. I sat in my too-hot car, and sobbed.

Here is the black T-shirt she wrote her name on in gold in nursery school.

I cry and I cry until the closet too is empty.

We did not allow the kids to eat upstairs. There was the mice problem. And my fear of them choking. And Lorne's fastidiousness. Still, I always suspected Grace snuck food upstairs. Sometimes she would be in her room and I'd stand in the doorway and ask her a question and she would keep her head turned from me. "Are you eating?" I asked her more than once. She always shook her head no.

But when I open the drawers of her bookshelf and begin to pull everything out, I find candy wrappers shoved in the back, half-eaten bags of jelly beans, an opened package of Peeps with two pink chicks still inside. I find this evidence and I start to laugh. I knew it! Of course it's ridiculous, but I feel like Grace left them there so even on this difficult day she can make me laugh.

I gather the crumpled wrappers into my hand and throw them away, and I am done. Grace's room, with the bed that has never been slept in, is completely empty of Grace.

"ISN'T IT FUNNY?" someone tells me. "People make shrines for Princess Diana and Jim Morrison, but they don't think you should keep your own child's things after she dies."

We line up Grace's shoes at the top of the stairs.

Sam gave her the red sparkly shoes for her fifth birthday because she had outgrown her gold sparkly ones.

She wore the pink metallic slip-ons during the entire three weeks our family traveled across Japan the August before she died. I bought them because we would have to take our shoes on and off so often there, and these had Velcro, and she could do it herself. Grace, who was so slow, always had her shoes off before the rest of us, and slipped into the Japanese slippers first.

When we got home from Japan, we went shopping for school shoes. The Skechers sneakers were purple and had Velcro too. But what Grace most loved about them was that they came with a small silver shoehorn. She liked to sit on the bottom step, slide her foot into the sneaker, and then insert the shoehorn to get the heel in just right.

She never got to wear the leopard boots. She was waiting for rain. But Grace loved leopard. Her backpack was leopard and her lunch box was leopard and she even had a leopard bathing suit when she was four. She got those boots for her fifth birthday. She pulled them on, walking clumsily because they were just a little bit too big. Lorne pulled her onto his lap and sat in the rocking chair he made back in high school. "Take our picture," he said, just as he did every year on her birthday. We imagined a lifetime of these pictures, Grace getting bigger and bigger each year, still happily posing on her father's lap. Her leopard boots swing happily to a stop. She faces the camera, and grins. That is the picture we brought to the ICU. *See,* that picture told all of those doctors and nurses, *Here is a unique and special child. Save her.*

But they couldn't.

That famous rabbi recited the Twenty-third Psalm for us that afternoon in his office. When he finished he said, "You see? The psalm tells us we walk *through* the valley of the shadow of death. Not around it or over it or beside it. *Through* it."

Time passes and I am still not through it. Grief isn't something you get over. You live with it. You go on with it lodged in you. Sometimes I feel like I have swallowed a pile of stones. Grief makes me heavy. It makes me slow. Even on days when I laugh a lot, or dance, or finish a project, or meet a deadline, or celebrate, or make love, it is there. Lodged deep inside of me. Time has passed and I am living a life again, back in the world.

At first, though, grief made me insane. It's true. I have been there. I am the one woman standing in the street on a Thanksgiving afternoon, screaming and pulling out my hair. That is my mother coming out the door, yelling my name. That is me, running from her, running down the beautiful street where houses wear plaques announcing how old and important they are. That is me making that sound which is both inhuman and guttural and the most human sound a person can make: the sound of grief. My hair is coming out, not in fistfuls, but in painful tangles, ripped from the root, from my scalp. That is me running, zigzagging, trying to escape what is inescapable: Grace is dead.

I HAVE BEEN THERE. That is me alone in the beautiful cemetery where important people are buried: Revolutionary War heroes, signers of famous documents, governors and senators. And Grace. My five-year-old daughter. We had to find a plot for her. We had to make decisions in the days after she died, when I still could not believe that she had died. Who could believe it? Five years old. Beautiful and funny and smart. And healthy. People came with questions that needed answers: What music did we want played at the service? What facts did we want in the newspaper? Did we want a viewing? Could we send clothes to the funeral home? Which Bible verses did we want read? Who would read them? Did we want a party of some kind afterward? Where did we want to bury our five-year-old daughter? *Here,* my husband said, and he drove me to that beautiful cemetery where a few weeks earlier he had taken Grace and Sam bike riding along its graceful, curving pathways beneath just-flowering dogwoods.

That is me the last afternoon I went there on my own: warm sun, the smell of dirt and flowers and heat. That is me, stepping from my car, walking on wobbly legs toward the spot that we chose. It is a blanket of dewy grass, freshly dug, freshly covered. That is me, the woman who is throwing herself on that spot, flinging her body down, and clawing at it, weeping. Dirt under my nails, grass in my mouth, hair wet with tears. That is me, vowing never to go back alone.

I HAVE BEEN THERE. I am the woman in dirty clothes that do not match, wearing flip-flops in the hard rain, crouched in her car, watching all the beautiful children leaving school. They are wearing bright slickers, rain boots that look like animals—frogs and ladybugs. They are clutching their mothers' hands. I am the woman who got special permission to park in the No Parking zone because the sight of all the little children makes me scream. My son emerges and runs up the walkway, across the small wooden bridge that stretches child-sized over a stream, up the grassy slope, to my car.

That is me trying to act normal for his sake. He slides into the backseat. His eyes meet mine in the rearview mirror. "So," he says, trying not show his worry, "what did *you* do today?" He is afraid that I have done nothing but cry or stare into space; or, even worse, sat for hours at the jigsaw puzzle of a European castle that I cannot stop working on, as if fitting those small jagged pieces together will solve something. "Me?" I say. "The usual boring stuff. More importantly, what did *you* do today?" Relieved, he tells me stories of immigration, stories of playground wars, recites the mid-Atlantic states and each of their capitals.

I AM THE WOMAN screaming at the airline ticket agent. I am trying to make plane reservations, a simple task that I cannot manage. There are schedules, choices, dates, and times. That is me screaming at the officious woman: *"My daughter is dead! My little girl is dead? Do you hear me? Do you?"*

THAT IS ME, crying in restaurants, in supermarkets, in traffic, in bed, at Christmas parties and dinner parties and school assemblies.

I HAVE BEEN THERE. At the brink of losing my mind. Unable to sleep for more than an hour or two. Unable to think of anything except what happened: how it happened, how it could have happened, why it happened. I ask my friends over and over how I could have stopped it, changed it, seen it coming. My mind only has these questions. Hospital images. My own screams echoing in it. I remember the great thirst that overcame me when she died. How I drank bottles and bottles of water in giant swallows, spilling it everywhere, gulping it, opening another bottle, guzzling that one, opening another. That thirst. I try to explain it, but it is only thirst after all. There are no answers for any of it.

I CANNOT SAY how I got from there to here. I cannot even say where "here" is. There are still nights when I cannot get rid of the images. Some mornings I still wake up crying, Grace's face large and close. Some days I do nothing but work a jigsaw puzzle: *See how the border takes shape? If I can only fill in the missing pieces,* I think. But then that passes and I break apart all that work and put it away.

Yet I am here, somewhere else. I am the woman with the cool vintage glasses, writing down the address of the shop in the East Village where I bought them. I am the one telling the funny story at dinner, making everyone laugh. I am the one throwing a party for two dozen people, everything done just right. I am the mother applauding her son as the Wolf in *Into the Woods,* as Augustus Gloop in *Charlie and the Chocolate Factory*, as Peter Cratchit in *A Christmas Carol.* I am the proud wife beside her husband at banquets and conferences and award ceremonies. I am the writer who has written a new novel, who has won a prize, who is teaching here and teaching there, who is standing in front of an audience at a bookstore and reading her new short story without faltering.

BUT DO NOT be fooled. I am not fooled. Even though I am here, I know that the smallest thing—a song, a sound, a smell—can send me back there.

I DO NOT live here. I only visit. Even as I stand here, charming, confident, smiling, I glimpse that other place. I stand always perched at the edge. I live in fear of the times when, without warning, I lift one foot, step from here, and go there, again.

CHAPTER TEN

Annabelle's Laughter

GRACE WAS BORN in the Year of the Rat. "Very clever," our Chinese nanny, Ju Hua, told us. "Very special." Those born in the Year of the Rat are sharp-witted and funny. They are charming too, and considered good luck. The Christmas Ju Hua was with our family, she had her husband in Beijing send Grace a gold charm of a small rat hanging on a chain. "Very special," Ju Hua explained. "Special present for a special girl."

Four months later, Grace died. Ju Hua and her daughter had moved into their own apartment by then. When they heard the news, they came immediately. Ju Hua's face was stricken, her crying uncontrollable. "That girl," she said. "So special."

Grace was studying Chinese at school, and even after Ju Hua left us, Grace would visit her and practice Chinese. "Her pronunciation so good!" Ju Hua would tell me when I picked Grace up. They had cooked together, fried rice and dumplings and the pork dish Grace liked so much. Smelling of garlic and sesame, Grace would wave goodbye to Ju Hua as we drove away. Then she would sing me a Chinese song, or count to twenty in Chinese.

That April day when Grace got sick and I rushed her to the emergency room, as they whisked her to the ICU, the doctor ordered me to help keep the oxygen mask on her face. "Grace," I said, trying to hide the fear that had gripped me, "count to ten and then you'll be in a room where the doctor can make you better."

Squirming under the oxygen mask, Grace began to count: *"Yee, uhr, sahn,"* she said in perfect Chinese, *"sah, woo, lyo . . ."*

When Ju Hua visited us after Grace died, she told us that her own mother had lost a child, a six-year-old boy. He got sick very suddenly, like Grace, and he died in her mother's arms as she walked miles to the doctor. "My mother never forget this," Ju Hua said. "But if he didn't die, I would never be born."

There are so many cruel decisions parents have to make when their child dies. The funeral director requested a sheet for the coffin, and I sent the cozy flannel one, pale blue with happy snowmen, that had just been put away with the winter linens. They needed clothes to bury her in, and I carefully removed the tags from the new capri pants with the ruffled hem and the pink shirt Grace had picked out but never got a chance to wear. We could, we were told, place anything we wanted in her coffin, so Lorne and I gathered her favorite things, the things that comforted her: Biff, her favorite stuffed animal; Cow, the green blanket decorated with cows; her purple leopard lunch box; her glasses; notes from each of us; crayons and paints; and the gold rat on the chain that Ju Hua had sent for her from China.

I CANNOT SAY for certain when the decision to have another child happened. I do remember sitting alone on a summer afternoon in the room we called the Puzzle Room, a room where Grace and Sam and I spent many afternoons listening to Nanci Griffith CDs and working on jigsaw puzzles, sitting there as the hot afternoon stretched endlessly and hopelessly before me, and thinking about how my arms ached to hold Grace and my entire body longed for the buzz of activity that used to surround me just a few short months earlier.

That first summer after Grace died, Lorne and I held each other through the seemingly endless nights and cried. But when morning came, I made myself get up, get dressed, and be the mother Sam had always had. I remembered when my own brother died and I felt I lost my mother as well. For the hours when Sam wasn't at camp or playing at a friend's we went on picnics or to the beach together. He held my hand extra hard during that time. Always theatrical, I watched him emerge as a clown, making me laugh even when I thought it was impossible, practicing his magic tricks on me, and crooning Broadway show tunes as we drove. When I did cry, he held me in his arms and cried with me, whispering, "I know, I know, I know."

It was that same summer that my husband and I camped out together on a beach in Maine and he said, "I have the craziest idea." "So do I," I told him. That was when I put words to it. "Let's have another baby," I said. And he said yes. Then we cried. Not a baby to replace Grace. Losing her had made it clear that she was, indeed, irreplaceable. But a baby to bring us joy again. To fill the long, sad hours when Lorne was at work and Sam was at school and I was left alone with my grief.

A light from a lighthouse kept swinging past us, illuminating everything.

FIRST, MY HUSBAND had to have his vasectomy reversed. Then, I had to have my hormone levels checked. I was forty-four years old, and I did not expect good news. But the doctor who everyone told us could help make it happen said that although I might need a little hormonal help, I could indeed get pregnant. When we told Sam what we were trying to do, he whooped with joy and gave me a fierce hug. Even at his age, he understood that we were trying to feel hope again.

Once a month, my husband and I drove to New York City to the doctor's Park Avenue office where Lorne masturbated into a cup and I was then inseminated with his sperm. Each time, the doctor was optimistic. Lorne's sperm were great—good swimmers and plentiful. I ovulated on schedule and had good mucous. We'd had babies before. We could do it again.

But after four months without a pregnancy, the doctor added Clomid to the protocol. I went for an intravaginal sonogram, my follicles were counted, and then we went to New York. Four eggs. Six. But no baby.

By March, I was having tests to see if something was going on. In June I had surgery to remove a benign polyp. By fall Lorne was injecting me with Pergonal at almost two thousand dollars a month, and it was producing fewer follicles than the Clomid, and I wasn't getting pregnant. Everyone has read about or knows someone who has gone through fertility treatments. It is an emotional nightmare, fueled by false hope and the promise of a treatment that will work. Add grief to that and the cycle gets even worse. By this time, I knew that bringing a baby into our household would help all of us. It would help ease the burden of our grief on Sam, who was only ten years old and read our emotions each morning like barometers. It would bring back the noise and laughter our house had lost. It would fill my empty hours. Babies make you do things for them. They get you up and they get you moving. A baby's smile, I knew, could change everything. But having a baby was beginning to seem unlikely.

One day, a friend told me that she knew how to get a baby in Russia, fast. It involved spending time in Finland. It would cost around forty thousand dollars, before bribes. The baby was a girl. She had red hair.

Another friend stopped by and told me that she could get children from Hungary. Not babies, but two- or three-year-olds. She could even get twins. Or siblings. It would cost sixty thousand dollars, plus donations to various people who would help along the way.

Some people urged me to give up the idea altogether. I heard stories of women who had a child after losing one and forced that new child into the roles of the dead one. I heard of mothers dressing their new baby in their dead child's clothes, making them swim or dance or whatever the other had done. It isn't fair, I was told. Fairness was not something I believed in very much then. If things were fair, a healthy, intelligent five-year-old girl wouldn't die. If things were fair, a family who helped others, who lived a good life together, who loved each other, wouldn't be torn apart like this.

I had spent almost twenty-five thousand dollars and I was out of expendable income. I realized that in this time that had passed and with the money I had spent, we could already have a red-haired baby from Russia, or three-year-old Hungarian twins. Lorne and I decided to stop the fertility treatments and focus on adoption instead. What I knew as soon as we made that decision was that in a year we would have a baby. By this time, grief had settled into our routine. We cried less, but the pain and Grace's absence loomed as large as ever. I could go out with friends and laugh at their jokes and foibles. I could sleep through the night most nights. But it was as if grief floated around us constantly, like Pigpen's cloud of dirt in the Peanuts cartoon.

Our talk turned to adoption. Again, Sam agreed readily. "Who cares how we get a baby," he said. "Let's just get one." Still, there were a few nights when, crying, he said what we all knew: "This baby won't be Grace. No one will." We talked about the idea of subsequent children, not replacement children, how this little person would be her own wonderful self and Grace would always be special, irreplaceable.

Once we began researching our possibilities, something settled in me. Somehow, this felt like the absolute right path for us. After talking to friends, and friends of friends, about their experiences adopting, we decided to adopt a baby girl from China. It is hard to explain how, in the midst of such overwhelming loss, I somehow knew that finally there was hope waiting for us again. Even knowing this was restorative after feeling so hopeless for so long.

FOR THE NEXT few months, I had coffee with women who had battled Central American governments, rescued children languishing in Russian and Romanian orphanages, lied, borrowed money, corrected cleft palates and crossed eyes and weak hearts, lost babies they had held, named babies they never got to see, traveled thousands of miles more than once, all in pursuit of a baby.

"I don't know if I have the emotional stamina for this," I told Lorne after hearing my friend's story about three failed adoptions in Guatemala and over a hundred thousand dollars spent. She did, finally, have her daughter. But still.

"China," Lorne said. "Everyone I talk to who adopted from China, it went like clockwork."

One afternoon I watched a mother at Sam's school pick up her daughter whom she had adopted from China. I sat in my car and watched that little girl leap into her mother's arms and I drove home and e-mailed that woman. As it turned out, she lived two blocks away from us. "Come over for coffee," she said, "and I'll tell you all about it."

Walking home from her house, Lorne squeezed my hand. "Let's start," he said.

Within a week we were sitting in a crowded room in an adoption agency office in Boston, signing papers, collecting information, beginning the journey that would lead us to China and a baby girl.

I spent the month of April 2004 filling out paperwork for the adoption. It was exactly two years since Grace had died. This process—collecting legal documents and getting fingerprinted and asking friends for recommendations—was the calmest, and most focused thing I had done in two years. I had a purpose, and I moved toward it with a doggedness I had forgotten I possessed.

What I didn't know was that while I filled out papers in triplicate and made appointments and arranged for a home study, a woman in Hunan, China, was giving birth to a baby girl she could not keep. Over a hundred thousand baby girls are abandoned every year in China. Some place the number at even higher than that. In Hunan, as in other provinces, infanticide is not uncommon. Some women give birth with a bucket of water by their beds, and if the baby is a girl, she is drowned. Other women walk for miles from their village to have their baby somewhere no one knows them. Baby girls are left on footbridges and in parks, at police station doors and orphanage entrances. They are left where their mothers know they will be found. It is illegal to abandon a baby in China, so they are left with no notes or pertinent information. In Hunan, a family who has a girl is allowed to have a second child. But that second child has to be a boy. Therefore, most of the abandoned baby girls in Hunan are second or even third daughters.

THE CALL WE waited almost a year for came on a rainy January morning. I was in Boston, comforting my lovesick cousin, when my cell phone started to ring. I ignored it. It rang some more. After a few rounds of this, I gave up and answered.

"Hon," my husband Lorne said, "Stephanie from the adoption agency is on the phone and she has news for us. I'm going to patch her in."

For the first time in almost three years, something like joy was creeping at the edges of my heart. I started to cry.

"I'm looking at a picture of your daughter,"

Stephanie said, and I cried harder. "She's adorable. And she looks really healthy."

By now, I was outright sobbing.

"She's nine months old," Stephanie said, and Lorne and I both managed to express delight and surprise; we had thought we might get an older baby.

And then Stephanie said: "Her birthday is April 18."

One of us gasped. I'm not sure which one. I think I said, "Oh no."

"Is there a problem?" Stephanie asked us.

I couldn't speak, but Lorne was able to tell her that, no, there was no problem. Everything was just fine, he said.

We made arrangements to go to the office and sign papers that very afternoon. Outside, cold rain pelted the windows.

"That birthday," I said when Stephanie was off the line.

"I know," Lorne said.

We were still both crying. But we made plans for Lorne to pick up our eleven-year-old son Sam at school and for us to meet at the adoption agency.

Then I hung up the phone and turned to my cousin. "We've got our baby."

Her Chinese name was Lou Fu Jing: Lou was the last name given to all the babies in her orphanage, which was in the city of Loudi; Fu was the name given to all the babies in her orphanage because it meant luck, and it was given to counter their bad luck; Jing was the name the orphanage gave her—bright. She lights up a room, an orphanage worker wrote on her referral papers.

Lorne and I had enlisted the opinions of both Sam and Lorne's fifteen-year-old daughter Ariane in the selection of the baby's name. I was leaning toward Tallulah and Lorne liked Lily. Somehow we had come up with a compromise of Mamie when Sam asked why we couldn't use Grace's middle name, Annabelle. "It's the prettiest name in the world," he added. "I want to name my own daughter Annabelle." Ariane agreed that it was her favorite name too. A name to honor Grace, a name we all loved. I looked at that face looking back at me and saw that she was, indeed, Annabelle.

When that call came on that rainy January day, my broken heart cried for my wonderful lost daughter, and for the new daughter I would hold soon. The agency gave us a picture of a beautiful round-faced baby wearing a pale pink sweater. Our Annabelle.

SEVEN WEEKS LATER, Lorne, Sam, and I flew to China to bring Annabelle home. Over the course of waiting, we had talked about this baby, how she was not ever meant to replace Grace. Rather, her arrival would herald a new beginning for our broken family. Since we had lost Grace, we had still found joy in each other: in Sam's many acting roles in theaters in our area; in Lorne's triumphant climb to the top of Mount Kiliminjaro, and in my own return to writing and teaching. But Annabelle, in that way that babies have, would open our hearts again.

Annabelle had been found in a box at the orphanage door, early in the morning of September 6, 2004. They estimated her age as five months. Most of the babies found abandoned are under two weeks old. Many of them still have their umbilical cord stump. No one will ever know what led Annabelle's mother to leave her there after five months. Perhaps she had not wanted to give her up at all. Perhaps a male relative waited until the baby was not nursing as much as a newborn does and then took her from her mother. Perhaps they tried to hide her in the system—a forbidden second or third daughter—and were caught. The penalties for this are huge, often involving many years' salary or loss of medical care for the entire family. Perhaps her mother died. Perhaps her mother got pregnant again and hoped for a boy.

We will never know what led to Annabelle being dressed in blue pants, white socks with blue flowers, a thin coat, and put into a cardboard box in a city that was most likely not her own. Around Loudi, there are dusty roads and fields of kale and sweet potatoes. Women walk with a bamboo pole across their backs, and one head of kale or a sweet potato in a basket at the ends. They take this meager yield to a market miles away to sell. It is not green or beautiful there. No mountains or sea, no glittering architecture. It is not the China in glossy magazines. It is poor and rural and the women there sometimes abandon their baby girls rather than drown them.

We will never know Annabelle's story. We only know this: the date they gave her as her birthday—determined by the age they guessed her to be on September 6, 2004; chosen as an even number because even numbers are lucky—that birthday, is April 18, the same day that Grace died. Annabelle, like me, was born in the Year of the Monkey. Monkeys are intelligent and are known to have a great sense of humor. Monkeys and rats are said to be the best of friends.

"THEY MARK THEM, you know," someone told us before we left for China. "The mothers brand the babies they abandon. It's a sign of love."

We had heard stories about babies being found with a yam, a sign of how valuable the baby was. We had heard of a note left that simply said: *This is my baby. Take care of her.* We had heard of one baby found with a bracelet around her wrist, and another with a river rock to indicate she was from a town near water. But this branding was something new.

The group of ten families with which we traveled to China all got our babies at the same time, in a nondescript city building in Changsha. Changsha is the capital of Hunan Province, and it is four hours from Loudi and the orphanage. Soon, people were lifting pant legs or the cuffs of sleeves to show the small scars on their babies. "They mark them," one mother said, spreading her new daughter's fingers to reveal a scar in between the index and pointer.

On Annabelle's neck I found a thick rope of scar tissue, round and small. The pediatrician examined it and frowned. "Don't get upset," he said, "but this almost looks like a burn that has healed."

Gingerly, I touched that small scar. If it was true that her birth mother had marked her, I felt only a kinship to that woman I would never know. We had both loved our daughters intensely. We had both lost our daughters. Annabelle's scar was visible, but her birth mother and I carried scars no one could see.

A few nights later, we flew from Changsha to Guangzhou for the final leg of our journey. Here, we would get the visa that would allow us to bring our babies into the United States. We would go to the American consulate and stand with our Chinese daughters as they became American citizens. On the bus from the airport in Guangzhou to our hotel, I held Annabelle in my lap. It was late. Many of the babies and the adults had fallen asleep. But Annabelle was still awake, smiling at me and tracing my face with her fingertips.

In the silence, she leaned back slightly and looked right at me. Then she tossed her head back and began to laugh. This was not the ordinary laughter she had been freely giving us. This laughter came from somewhere deep inside her. If joy has a sound, it is the sound of Annabelle's laughter. That night, it was as if Annabelle realized that she had found the right family. And for me, holding her, listening to her laughter, it was as if the entire universe was telling us that we had found each other.

WE ARRIVED BACK home to Providence on April 6, 2005. It was the Year of the Rooster. In Chinese astrology, there is an improvement in difficult situations during rooster years. They are a time to seek emotional solace. One of the hexagrams of the I Ching that symbolizes the middle third of a rooster year—the time when Mother's Day falls—

is the image of a small trickle of water flowing from a rock as a container below it slowly begins to fill. It is called "the humble power of the smallest."

BACK IN MAY OF 2002, a month after Grace died, I had my first Mother's Day without my daughter. Sam and Lorne carved a heart out of wood, sanded it smooth as if they could ease the pain in my own heart this way. They threaded the wooden heart on a dark red ribbon, and it still hangs from the rearview mirror of my car. But Lorne also gave me a book he made, with pictures of Grace and descriptions beneath them of what Grace and I did together: cooking, reading, laughing, walking hand in hand. It was the worst Mother's Day I could imagine. Here was Sam, my son, offering me a heart. And here was the empty chair, the silence, my own heart, broken.

Each subsequent Mother's Day brought a new pain—the passing of time without watching Grace growing up, the burst of spring blossoms in our garden mocking my loss. I was a daughterless mother. I had nowhere to put the things a mother places on her daughter. The nail polish I used to paint our toenails hardened. Our favorite videos gathered dust. Her small apron was in a box in the attic. Her shoes—the sparkly ones, the leopard rainboots, the ballet slippers—stood in a corner. I kept her hairbrush on a shelf in my closet, and the fine strands of her pale blonde hair were still tangled in it. As I walked out the door, I still sometimes paused to bury my nose in her powder blue jacket, as if I might find something of her there.

Three Mother's Days later, I am sitting in my kitchen singing to Annabelle. It is raining, and I am singing an old Lovin' Spoonful song . . . "You and Me and Rain on the Roof" . . . I am singing to Annabelle and she is grinning at me, a big toothless grin. When Annabelle laughs, my heart soars. When she presses her hand into mine, or rests her head against my chest, or falls asleep in my arms, I feel myself slowly, slowly coming back to life.

Sometimes I touch that small round scar on her neck and I wonder about the woman who might have put it there. I wonder if she walked down those dusty roads I saw in China, past the endless fields of kale, cradling her daughter in her arms. I wonder if she cried when she placed her in that small box. I wonder what words she might have whispered to her. They were, I imagine, no different from the words I whispered to Grace in that ICU.

IT SOUNDS CLICHÉD to say that after having Annabelle for only a few months, it feels like forever, but that is truly the way it feels. When Sam walks into the room, she lifts her arms toward him so he can swoop her into his own. She flirts with Lorne, and places wet kisses on my cheeks.

"How does it feel to have a daughter?" people who don't know me well ask.

I swallow hard. I want to scold them, to make sure they know that I had a daughter, an amazing, funny, smart girl named Grace; that Annabelle is my second wonderful daughter. But usually I just smile and tell them it's great. Because it is great.

One afternoon, as I strapped Annabelle into her car seat, a feeling of overwhelming grief filled me. I missed Grace, just like I do every day. Even as tears sprang to my eyes, I was smiling, happy at the sight of Annabelle grinning up at me, showing off her two new teeth. The feelings of grief and joy live side by side now in my heart. I did not know that they, such opposites, could coexist.

But they do. Perhaps never more so than this year on April 18. Just as I have for the past three years, as the day approached, I began to remember all of the small things that led up to it. As I walked down our street, lined with dogwoods in full bloom, I could almost picture Grace skipping ahead of me, Sam on his scooter beside her. "Stop at the corner!" I always called after them, afraid of cars darting out of alleys, or the mean pugs from the house on the corner running loose, or any of the dangers that threatened them. Or I see the purple blanket of myrtle, the slender stalks of chives, and picture Grace's head bent, her glasses slipping to the tip of her nose, as she picks them for me. I remember how hot it was that year, Grace's delight that I let the neighbor's orange cat come in for a nap, her throaty laughter as she ate thin rounds of cucumber, fistfuls of blueberries, and guzzled milk from her baby bottle still.

I cried when I woke up that morning, the ache for Grace like a hole punched in my heart. At the cemetery, we brought pink flowers to her grave, and sat on the green grass crying together.

That evening, Annabelle sat in her high chair, grinning as we raised a cake high, a big colorful *1* ablaze in the center, and sang "Happy Birthday" to her. Afterward, she lifted her arms to me. I picked her up and pressed my nose into the nape of her neck, the place where babies smell best. I held her close, letting joy slowly, finally, fill me. I held her, oh, so close.

I HAVE HAD five Mother's Days without Grace now. And on each subsequent one, I think of her. And I think about this woman I will never know. I, of course, thank her, and I praise her strength in doing this seemingly impossible thing: giving her daughter to me. She will never know that I have her daughter because I lost Grace. She will never know the road I traveled to get her.

This Mother's Day, I lay in bed feeling that strange mixture of grief and joy. Down the hall, I heard Annabelle's high, squeaky voice and Lorne's lower one. I picture Grace in her smudged glasses, her tangled hair, her wry smile. I feel tears building in my eyes, even as I hear Lorne and Annabelle's futile efforts to make Sam wake up. Then there are footsteps, and Annabelle is at the side of the bed, clutching a pink rose.

"Happy Mother's Day," she says, grinning.

Annabelle lifts her arms to me, and I pick her up.

"Mama," she whispers.

"Daughter," I whisper back.

EPILOGUE

Today

TODAY IS MAY 19, 2006, four years, one month, and one day since Grace died. I used to wake in a panic that I had forgotten even one detail about her, or that I would forget someday. Now I know that will not happen. I remember everything. I remember how she used to yell at Sam when she was angry with him: "Sorry isn't good enough, Sam!" I remember how she felt climbing into my lap after she finished dinner, sitting there while I finished mine. I remember everything. It is all I have of her. I remember.

It seems like as soon as she died, people were urging me to write about her, about losing her, about grief. People told me I could help others. People told me that I could make sense of loss. But, of course, I can't. No one can. There is no sense to it.

People send me names and addresses and details of horrible losses, children drowning, dying in car accidents, getting unnamed viruses that ravage them. I write them notes. I offer help. I cook them dinner. I listen. I feel guilty that in the end, I don't feel like I have helped them. How can I? How can anyone? Their child is dead. What can I do or say to change that? I teach grieving mothers to knit. I let them tell me in excruciating, painful, and desperate detail what happened that afternoon, that night, that snowy day.

I only know this: someday they will find themselves, as I do today, four years, one month, and one day later living life without their child. At some distant point in the future, they will find themselves sitting at a table looking out at a rainy May morning, drinking coffee, noticing how green everything is, delighting in a glimpse of a bright red cardinal, getting ready to peel a ripe orange and enjoy each juicy wedge.

Today I will drive my car to the grocery store and buy milk and coffee and fruit. I will browse in a bookstore. I will sing along with the radio. Someday, all of these parents will find themselves doing these ordinary things too.

I remember when I used to pick up Grace from kindergarten every day at two o'clock. She went to a school called the Montessori Children's House and it was, indeed, an old Victorian house on a tree-lined street with a big front porch. Parents parked in front of the house and then waited on the porch for their child to emerge. One of the teachers stood in the open front doorway and called to each child as her parent appeared. "Grace Adrain," she'd say over her shoulder, and that was Grace's cue to put on her coat and grab her lunch box and backpack and run to me. Whenever I saw her coming through that door, my heart skipped a beat, and I opened my arms and swooped her up; she was still little enough for me to hold her easily in a hug.

In the car, she slid into the backseat, fastened her

seat belt, and handed forward all of her papers, her careful practicing of writing letters and numbers, her Weekly Reader all filled in, a piece of art. I watched her from the rearview mirror as she unloaded that big leopard backpack of hers. She'd catch my eye and grin at me. "Learning to read is hard work," she told me one day about a week before she died. She would then reach forward to the spot where I kept a baby bottle of warm milk, an indulgence of hers still. As we drove toward Sam's school, I'd glance in the mirror, laughing to myself at this girl, so grown-up in so many ways, enjoying a bottle with such relish. Once, a boy from school spotted her and shouted: "You still drink from a bottle!" And Grace only smiled at him and waved happily, unaffected by his disdain.

I realize now how often I picture her that way, sweaty and tired from a long day of kindergarten. Happy to be in the car with me. Happy to be picking up Sam. Happy to be headed home. I realize that this is how mothers see their children: through the rearview mirror. We are moving forward, but watching them behind us. Not growing smaller, but smiling, happily, at us.

At Grace's school every morning when the teacher took attendance, the children responded to their names with: "Here I am!" The teacher would say, "Grace Adrain," and Grace would call out: "Here I am!"

I sit here today, four years, one month, and one day since Grace died. Since I've seen her. Since I've held her. Since I've heard her funny, throaty voice. I have a broken heart. I am writing a book. I am drinking my coffee. It is raining outside. The grass is very green. A cardinal flies away. I think of my daughter, my Gracie Belle. I say: "Grace, here I am." I say, "Here I am." And I hope, I pray, that somehow she hears.

acknowledgments

With gratitude and love to all those who offered—who still offer—comfort: my mother, Gloria Hood; my aunts, uncles, cousins, and niece; the Adrains; the Bourgeois/Stenhouses, the Coopers, the Cox/Russows, the Emmonses, the Foxes, the Greens, the Handys, the Ingendahls, the Lietars, the Lupicas, the Majorises, the Minkin/Stones, the Neels, the Pines, the Rosenbergs, the Schulman/Handys, the Sloane/Wallersteins, the Thachers; Matt Davies,

Hillary Day, Elizabeth Gregory, and Heather Watkins; Jill Bialosky, Paul Whitlatch; Diane Higgins; Gail Hochman; FOFA; Dr. Therese Rando; Sam and Pat Smith and June and Ray Vincent; Joanne Brownstein, Marianne Merola; Maya Ziv; The Corporation of Yaddo; the teachers and families at the Gordon School and the Montessori Children's House; the families of Compassionate Friends; everyone at Sakonnet Purls, especially Jen Silverman; everyone at the All Children's Theatre; Poo White and Karla Harry; the Wildacres community; my wonderful editors at *Alimentum, Good Housekeeping, Ladies' Home Journal, More,* the *New York Times, O, Parents, Real Simple, Redbook,* and *Tin House* where many of these words found early homes; the editors of the anthologies where much of this appeared; and of course my husband Lorne Adrain and our wonderful children Sam, Annabelle, Ariane, and Grace.

Joyce Ravid

Ann Hood is the author of nine books, including the novels *The Knitting Circle*, *Somewhere Off the Coast of Maine*, and *Ruby*, and the story collection *An Ornithologist's Guide to Life*. She has won a Pushcart Prize and a Best American Spiritual Writing Award, as well as the Paul Bowles Prize for Short Fiction. Her essays and stories have appeared in *The Paris Review*, *Tin House*, *O Magazine*, and elsewhere. She lives in Providence, Rhode Island.

Her website is www.annhood.us.

A Note from Ann Hood

When my five-year-old daughter Grace died suddenly from a virulent form of strep in April of 2002, I searched desperately for a book that offered validation for my grief and some comfort for my broken heart. When I could not find one that did both, I vowed that if I ever could write about this enormous and unspeakable loss, I would honor Grace and all of us who have suffered losses by writing an honest, searing, yet hopeful book. The emails I have received since *Comfort* was published have told me that my own loss, and the words I have written about it, have reached people who—like me—strive to make sense of life, struggle to get through another day, and seek understanding and comfort. Daily, I am honored and moved by readers and their willingness to share their own stories. These are just a few of the words that have brought me comfort.

Excerpts from emails sent to Ann's Web site:

"Your book, *Comfort*, chose me at the library. I tried putting it back on the shelf several times. I wrote down the title and promised to check it out another time. But it insisted on going home with me today. When I got home I sat down and read it cover to cover, nodding my head, saying, Yes, that's exactly how it is. My thirty-six-year-old daughter died on February 9, 2007, after a two-and-a-half-year battle with cancer. When I sat in the chemo room with her I often thought about mothers who have to watch young children suffer and die. How much more horrible that would be. The grief is the same, though. And your book lets me know I am not crazy. Thank you, thank you for writing again and for sharing your pain so honestly."

—Deborah Pace

"I love your book for being an honest, heart-wrenching tribute to someone you love more than your own life. . . . You write beautifully, right to my heart." —Annie Dill

"Aidan Sophia, our granddaughter . . . died at the age of four months, on October 20, 2005. . . . She had open heart surgery, which she survived, but following that she needed to be put on a heart-lung machine. . . . She had strokes and massive bleeding in the brain. . . . So I know all too well the truth in your book. I started crying with the prologue and I haven't really stopped yet, but the crying is the cathartic kind—the kind you get when you meet someone who knows your grief." —Marcia Hunt

"I have not had a child die, but have had two granddaughters die. Without a doubt, *Comfort* is the best expression of this deepest of griefs. You pull no punches, spare no emotion, express your extreme loss and love for Grace in almost poetic style." —Jack McCarron

"I, too, lost my only daughter. She was twenty-six and we had just bought her wedding dress. She was an amazing person—beautiful, compassionate, smart, funny. The way you write about the loss is so real for me I want to jump up and scream—Yes!! This is how it is!! This is just how I feel and it must be OK because you felt it, too! . . . Thank you for your book, for expressing the feelings that are so in common with mothers who have to go through this. I have read shelves of books on grieving but none connected with me like this." —Lynn Liedman

"Thank you so much for your gift of writing. *Comfort* let me know that I am not alone and that I can go on."

—Carolyn Sweet

"Your book is the closest thing I have found to explaining what I have experienced and what I feel." —Neil Mufson

"I lost my daughter six years ago this November. She was eight years old. I didn't realize where I was in the grieving process until I read this book. . . . You certainly explained some of the sorrow that I have been experiencing. I was able to step back and remember that others have pain as deep as mine, and I'm not alone." —Cindy Seguin